# PRACTICAL
# WOODWORKING

A STEP-BY-STEP GUIDE TO WORKING WITH WOOD, WITH OVER
60 TECHNIQUES AND A FULL GUIDE TO TOOLS, SHOWN IN 650
EASY-TO-FOLLOW COLOUR PHOTOGRAPHS AND DIAGRAMS

D1463418

**STEPHEN CORBETT**

HERMES HOUSE

This edition is published by Hermes House

Hermes House is an imprint of Anness Publishing Ltd
Hermes House, 88–89 Blackfriars Road, London SE1 8HA
tel. 020 7401 2077; fax 020 7633 9499

www.hermeshouse.com; www.annesspublishing.com

If you like the images in this book and would like to investigate using them for
publishing, promotions or advertising, please visit our website
www.practicalpictures.com for more information.

Publisher: Joanna Lorenz
Managing editor: Judith Simons
Project editor: Felicity Forster
Editor: Ian Penberthy
Designer: James Lawrence
Illustrator: Julian Baker
Photographer: John Freeman
Stylist: Annie le Painter
Contributors: Andrew Gillmore, Bob Cleveland
Production controller: Don Campaniello

ETHICAL TRADING POLICY
Because of our ongoing ecological investment programme, you, as our customer, can
have the pleasure and reassurance of knowing that a tree is being cultivated on your
behalf to naturally replace the materials used to make the book you are holding. For
further information about this scheme, go to www.annesspublishing.com/trees

© Anness Publishing Ltd 2003, 2007

A CIP catalogue record for this book is available from the British Library.

Previously published as part of a larger volume, *The Practical Woodworker.*

Publisher's note
The author and the publisher have made every effort to ensure that all instructions contained
in this book are accurate and that the safest methods are recommended. The publisher and
author cannot accept liability for any resulting injury, damage or loss to persons or property
as a result of using any tools in this book or carrying out any of the projects. Before you
begin any woodworking task, you should know how to use all your tools and equipment
safely and that you are sure and confident about what you are doing.

# Contents

# INTRODUCTION

BY OPENING THIS BOOK, you have already displayed the first qualification to proceed further – a basic interest in wood and how it is used. Millions of people share this interest, and all of us benefit to some degree from its use. This book itself is made from paper, a universal product derived from the same raw material that goes into our houses, our furniture and many other items that we come into contact with daily. Despite the undoubted progress made by humankind in the development of metals, alloys, synthetic resins and plastics, wood, in its natural form, has been a part of our lives for thousands of years and will remain so.

## Why wood?

Wood has a universal and appealing presence to every culture and country. As a constructional material is invaluable and very strong for its weight. It can be used to create complex structures at relatively low cost. Properly looked after timber (lumber) will last for years, as an examination of your surroundings will confirm.

Centuries of woodworking tradition have refined the techniques and tools we currently use, allowing a multitude of uses and styles. Best of all, wood is a sustainable resource – well managed woodlands can produce an inexhaustible supply of raw material, as well as playing a vital part in a balanced environment. Imagine

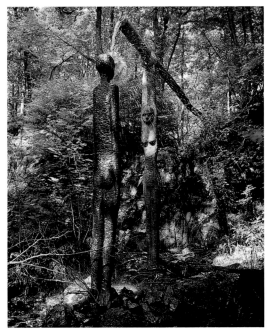

*Above* Houses being constructed from timber (lumber).
*Left* Wood has been used for sculpture for centuries. Here is a showering couple in the Grizedale Forest, Hawkshead, UK.
*Opposite* Wood is strong, attractive and in furniture joints can be used as a decorative feature in a design.

asking modern technologists to invent a synthetic material with so many qualities. Then ask them to add other properties – to make it feel warm and alive to the touch, and to look attractive at the same time.

The secret of being a successful woodworker or furniture maker lies in understanding that wood, as an organic material, was once alive, and that it can live again when shaped and formed by the human hand. No two pieces of wood are ever the same, and appreciating the variation will allow you to make the most of the material's natural qualities. All the tools and techniques in the world will be of no use without this feel for the material, which every woodworker shares.

When you have made your first piece of work, try this simple test – show it to someone else and wait for them to reach out and touch it. Then you will know that you have become part of a tradition of craftsmanship that will always be with us, and that you have taken the first step on a rewarding journey that has no end.

## The purpose of this book

The following pages provide a guide to the raw materials, tools, fixings, fittings and techniques that you need to be familiar with before perfecting the art of woodworking.

Recognizing and selecting the right kind of timber (lumber) is the first step to successful design and construction, and the book begins with a section describing how softwoods and hardwoods behave when worked by hand or machine tools, the quality of the grain, and how they take to different adhesives and finishes. Each type of wood has particular advantages and disadvantages, so it is important to choose carefully.

Using the right tools for the job is an equally important consideration, and the book provides a detailed guide to the various families of tools, what they do and which ones you should think about buying. Rather than purchasing a cheap "beginner's" toolkit, it is better to start with a few good-quality tools and expand your collection as the need arises. Similarly, your store of fixings and fittings will grow according to the projects you work on over the years.

The techniques sections of the book provides a good grounding for improving your skills and expertise. From cutting and shaping to making joints and polishing, all the most common woodworking methods are covered.

Taking short-cuts and making choices without exploring all the options can produce quicker results, but woodworking is not a race against time. Patience is one of the primary attributes of any good craftsperson. Take the trouble to consult each chapter in turn, using the information as the foundation of a thorough and sympathetic understanding of each task you approach.

There is no substitute for experience, and that is what you will find distilled in these pages. What you will not find is the reward that comes from your own efforts – the key to this lies in your own hands, and the understanding of the tools and materials you use.

## Note on measurements

Making accurate measurements is one of the most important skills to acquire if you want to achieve good results. The task can be made more confusing by the fact that different countries and timber suppliers work to different standards, using either the metric or imperial system (or sometimes a combination of the two), when sizing the raw material.

The same applies to tool manufacturers and suppliers of fixings and hardware. The way through this maze is to develop an understanding of both systems until mental conversion becomes second nature. A pocket calculator will help, but actually can slow the process.

In this book, dimensions are given in both metric and imperial form, but you should always check that the accuracy of any conversion is sufficient for the task in hand. Fractions of an inch, or 1 or 2 millimetres, either way are less critical in gauging large quantities of timber than when setting out detail, and converted values are often rounded up or down to make life easier. The table shown below provides some useful conversion factors and short-cut methods for estimating larger quantities of wood.

### Conversion table

| Multiply | by | to obtain | short-cuts |
|---|---|---|---|
| inches | 25.4 | millimetres | divide by four and add two zeros (4in = 100mm) |
| feet | 305 | millimetres | multiply by three and add two zeros (1ft = 300mm) |
| square feet | 0.093 | square metres | divide by ten |
| cubic feet | 0.028 | cubic metres | divide by 35 (35cu ft = 1cu metre) |
| lb/cu ft | 16.05 | kg/cu m | add two zeros, divide by six |
| pounds | 0.45 | kilograms | divide by two and subtract 10% (2.2lb = 1kg) |

# WOOD

**T**o most people, wood comes ready to use from a timber (lumber) yard or home improvement store, cut to standard lengths and planed to a smooth finish. Modern processing and marketing practices demand that the natural variation of the product is eliminated as far as possible. But wood is not a manufactured material, and its qualities are as varied as the trees from which it is derived.

As a discriminating woodworker, you will soon discover that the real pleasure of woodworking comes from exploring the potential of each species and using it to its best advantage. The knowledge and careful selection of the raw material is one of the most important steps to take in developing a feel for your craft. This chapter describes the immense variety and options available to you as the living tree is processed to arrive in usable form at your workbench.

# THE RAW MATERIAL

Trees are arguably the most prominent members of the plant kingdom. They have been around for millions of years, forming a vital part of the natural biological cycle that keeps this planet alive. Like all plants, they depend on a process called photosynthesis to harness the sun's energy, combine it with carbon dioxide ($CO_2$) from the air and produce the nutrients they need to grow. In return, oxygen is emitted to the atmosphere and vast quantities of water evaporate from the leaves.

## Tree trunks

The most useful and important part of the tree is the trunk, or bole. This performs three roles: it conducts water, or sap, from the roots; it supports the weight of the tree; and it stores the nutrients produced in the leaves to lay down new growth. Different parts of the trunk are adapted to each function, but all use the same basic building blocks: the cells, which have walls made of cellulose, the raw material of wood. When pulped and processed, cellulose can be made into paper; when it is left intact, it provides one of the most versatile constructional materials available.

*Above* A western yellow pine *(Pinus ponderosa)*, a softwood species, in spring.
*Opposite top* A Californian redwood, a softwood species, *(Sequoia sempervirens)*.
*Opposite below* Mature oaks, a temperate hardwood species, *(Quercus robur)*, from a post-Napoleonic-war plantation.

### Living cycle within the tree

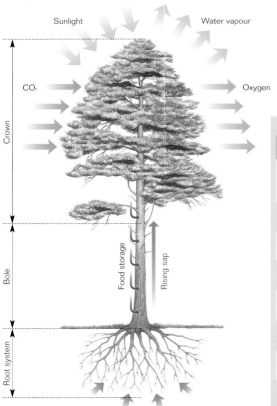

Sunlight

Water vapour

$CO_2$

Oxygen

Crown

Food storage

Rising sap

Bole

Root system

### Timber properties

| Softwoods | Hardwoods |
| --- | --- |
| low density: 400–600kg/cu m (25–37lb/cu ft) | high density: up to 1,000kg/cu m (65lb/cu ft) |
| great strength with lighter weight | heavier and sometimes more brittle |
| less durable in wet or damp conditions | more suitable for exterior use |
| less resistance to insect attack | more resistant to decay and rot |
| generally pale colouring | light to very dark colouring |
| generally more open grained | close-grained and harder to work |
| tendency to shrink or swell | more stable |
| low cost and more readily available | more expensive and harder to obtain |

flexibility, brittleness, and, of course, appearance. Understanding these qualities will help you select the best material for the job in hand. One of the first choices to make is not as straightforward as it may seem – softwood or hardwood?

Trees are divided into two botanical groups: *Gymnosperms* and *Angiosperms*, or conifers and broadleaves. These groups are popularly and respectively known as softwoods and hardwoods, but the terms can be misleading. Some so-called softwoods from coniferous trees, such as yew and pitch pine, are considerably harder than certain tropical hardwoods, not least balsa wood, which is the lightest of all.

The strength of timber (lumber) is determined by its density, which can vary within the same species according to its country of origin and rate of growth. Conifers are concentrated primarily in the cooler regions of the world, in both the northern and southern hemispheres, while tropical hardwoods, as the name implies, are found in the equatorial belt.

A third group, the temperate hardwoods, occupies the middle zone and is of special interest to woodworkers. Great variation can be found in the colour, distinctive grain figure and working properties of this group, and commercial supplies from sustainable sources are readily available at reasonable cost.

Whatever group timber belongs to, the woodworker will want to know its workability: how it behaves when worked by hand or machine tools, the quality of the grain, and how it takes to different adhesives and finishes. For most practical purposes, the more commonly available commercial softwoods all have certain similar features, with particular advantages and disadvantages as you can see in the table opposite.

**Softwoods and hardwoods**
Depending on the species and conditions of growth, wood possesses a wide range of characteristics in varying degrees: strength, durability,

# STRUCTURE OF WOOD

**A good woodworker does not have to be an expert in botany, or even dendrology (the study of trees), but it does help to have a basic knowledge of a tree's internal structure. This allows the selection of the best material for the job at hand and assists in spotting potential defects, which can show up and spoil the finished product.**

### Drying wood

An important part of the design process is knowing how wood behaves as it is worked and as it dries, which can vary depending on the part of the tree from which it originates. The cutaway section below of a tree trunk shows the principal elements that are common to most commercially available softwoods and temperate hardwoods.

### The layers of a tree trunk

The outer layer is the *bark* of the tree, which protects it as it grows. Just beneath the bark is the *bast*, a vital part of the tree's make-up. It conducts the sugars manufactured in the leaves down toward the base of the tree for storage, while the narrow *cambium* alongside it is responsible for creating new growth each year. The outer

layers are attractive to pests in search of the food products they contain, so most of the seasoned timber (lumber) supplied for woodworking will have had them removed at an early stage.

In the *sapwood* layer, each year's new growth is laid down and the cells conduct the sap upward from the root system. In some species, the sapwood is distinct, being pale in colour, while in others there is no visible barrier between sapwood and *heartwood*. Sapwood has the same strength as heartwood, but is more vulnerable to attack by furniture beetle, so as a rule it should be cut away. It can develop unsightly greyish-blue stains and is porous, making good glued joints and smooth finishes difficult to obtain.

The heartwood makes up the bulk of the tree and is the most usable part.

*Above* Growth rings are clearly visible in the end grain of these boards.

The cells of the heartwood are not alive, but they provide all the strength of the tree. As the tree grows, sapwood becomes heartwood, which is more durable and often of a darker colour. Each year's new growth forms another layer, and these rings enable the age of the tree to be determined.

In many species, especially from temperate climates where there is a distinct growing season every year, the rings are clearly visible, giving rise to an attractive striped grain figure. When a board is cut radially, through the growth rings to the centre, the *rays* will be revealed in cross-section. These run horizontally through the tree, storing food deposits as it increases in girth. They are very visible in oak, producing a characteristic silvery band; in other species, they are barely detectable by the naked eye.

The *pith*, at the very core of the trunk, is the oldest part of the tree; however, it is not the strongest. It is the growth laid down when the tree is immature, and it is softer and less durable than the true heartwood. It can flake out when being worked, and is prone to decay and uneven shrinkage as the wood dries. Defects can arise at the centre of the pith, and often it is removed when the log is processed.

### The structure of wood

Growth rings

Rays

Bark

Bast Cambium

Sapwood

Heartwood

Pith

Radial section

Tangential section

## Wood grain

Some species of timber (lumber) are termed straight-grained, where the growth rings are tight and concentric around the heart of the tree; they are a pleasure to work with.

*Above* These American white oak boards display the attractive striped grain figure common to woods with distinct growth rings. They have been cut tangentially – that is, cut across the face of the growth rings to reveal the cone-shaped formation.

## Knots

A knot is simply the remains of a branch where it grew from the main trunk of the tree, but it should not always be regarded as a defect. Small knots can create interesting effects in an otherwise bland piece of timber.

*Above* This panel of black walnut contains a good example of a dead knot. The small "pin" knot lower down creates an attractive pattern, but the large dead knot above it is a defect to be avoided.

However, they do cause problems when working the wood, and joints and fine detail should be positioned away from them if possible. A dead knot, encased in a ring of bark where a dead branch has been absorbed by the growing tree, should be avoided. It is likely to shrink and fall out, and, in softwoods particularly, can be very resinous, causing problems when applying a finish.

## Defects

Short- or cross-grain defects still occur, however, as a result of uneven growth or the grain being deformed around a knot. Very short or close grain is almost impossible to work successfully with hand tools without it tearing. It drastically weakens the material and should be avoided for constructional members and sections of wood close to joints. Certain species, particularly some tropical hardwoods, can always be expected to have difficult grain, growing naturally in spiral or interlocking patterns.

*Above* In this panel of European beech, the rays appear as small oval flecks distributed liberally across the face of the timber.

## Shakes and checks

Heart shake

Ring shake

Surface checks

## Reaction wood

This occurs where uneven growth in the trunk of the tree puts the fibres under great pressure. It can be identified by tight bands of growth rings that are much darker than their surroundings. These areas are much weaker, more difficult to work and subject to abnormal movement or shrinkage. Large areas of reaction wood should be cut out when selecting stock.

*Above* Sapele is an example of a hardwood with a difficult grain, the alternate formation of each band of cells producing a striped effect. The right-hand panel in this photograph not only shows unacceptable short grain, but also another defect known as reaction wood.

## Shakes and checks

Small fissures, or *checks*, in the outer surface of a sample are not serious. Of greater concern are *shakes*, which arise within the tree due to decay or high stresses, or even old age. Star-shaped *heart shakes* can develop in the centre of a tree that has passed maturity. *Ring shakes* form between the growth rings and can be caused by the shock of being felled. A board with these defects should be rejected – it is unsound and will only deteriorate.

# PRODUCTION AND CONVERSION

**Imagine a tree with a trunk that is 610mm (2ft) in diameter, with a useful length of 12m (40ft) stretching up toward the crown. This represents a volume of timber (lumber) of 3.5cu m (124cu ft). Imagine a billion such trees and you will have an idea of worldwide timber consumption in a year. Not all of this is converted into useful wood products, however – in fact, more than half is burned for fuel. Much of the remainder is converted into wood pulp for the paper and packaging industries.**

*Above* Resawing an oak board to remove the heart shake.

*Below* A typical log storage yard.

### Tree felling

Timber production is a massive global industry, and the route taken by a piece of wood before it reaches your workbench is complex and varied. The home woodworker has a vast range of options available when specifying the correct quality and form of material to give the best results and reduce waste.

From the moment a tree is selected for felling, it is subjected to a continual process of evaluation to grade its quality and most useful content. When it reaches the sawmill, it will be allowed to "rest" for a period to allow the natural tensions within

the trunk to equalize, before being converted into large slabs for seasoning. A skilled operator will know how to convert the log into the greatest quantity of usable timber with the minimum of waste.

As with most things, the higher the quality of product, the higher the cost, and the way in which the log is converted into convenient sizes can affect this dramatically.

Understanding the different methods and terminology will help you to specify the correct type of wood for your needs, and predict its behaviour under different conditions. The appearance of the cut surface,

the amount of waste and the way in which the wood shrinks as it loses moisture are all affected by the conversion method.

The quickest and least wasteful method of converting the log, or baulk, of timber is to make a series of parallel cuts along its length. This process is known as through and through cutting, sometimes abbreviated to T/T.

## Through and through cutting

This style of cutting is normal for most large-scale commercial sawmills. It produces large quantities of boards with a tangential figure, the cuts being made across the growth rings and producing the familiar cone-shaped pattern on the face of each board.

Such boards are described as plain sawn, flat sawn or slash sawn. Many species of wood with distinctive or contrasting growth rings are shown to their best advantage when converted in this way. To maximize the yield of highly figured boards, the entire baulk can be plain sawn.

*Above* Sawing a prime ash log on a bandmill.

Plain sawn board

Through and through cutting

Growth rings

Plain sawn

*Above* Quarter sawing oak on a bandmill.

## Quarter sawing

In contrast, when a log is cut into quarters, and sawn radially, at right-angles to the growth rings, with the cut passing through the centre, the figure displayed is markedly different.

The photograph on the right shows a good example of quarter-sawn oak, the silky blaze of the rays being clearly visible in cross-section and the growth rings reduced to fine parallel lines. As the diagram below shows, however, this method is wasteful of timber and time-consuming, since the log needs regular repositioning on the saw table. True quarter-sawn timber, with the cut surface intersecting the growth rings at a right

angle, is only produced when the quality or the decorative value of the timber warrants it.

Boards described as quarter sawn from the supplier will have been cut by one of several methods, as shown. These are a compromise and accept the rings running at any angle of more than 45 degrees from the face.

Another possibility is rift-sawn boards, where the log is split horizontally, then sawn through and through vertically to produce boards with a higher proportion of quartered grain. Sometimes this is described as one square edge and it can yield good-quality material at a much lower cost.

*Above* A fine example of black walnut, with a plain-sawn panel on the left, quarter-sawn on the right and rift-sawn in the centre. The changing angle of growth rings across the panel can be seen clearly.

Quarter sawn

Quarter-sawn board

Rift sawn

True quarter sawn

Ray

Commercially quarter sawn

# SEASONING WOOD

**Newly felled timber (lumber) loses moisture rapidly at first as free water evaporates, then more slowly as water within the cell walls is given up. The woodworker should look for well-seasoned timber, which will have been dried at the sawmill under controlled conditions in two distinct stages.**

*Above* This shows how not to air dry timber. The boards have been piled in irregular fashion, unprotected from the heat of the sun. Rapid, uneven drying can split a board quite easily. Note the discolouration where the sticks were laid.

## Shrinkage

When newly felled, timber has a high water content and is termed "green". It is heavier and more vulnerable to decay than seasoned timber. However, it can be worked quite easily and is more flexible. As it dries, it will shrink slightly and can distort in shape.

The cherrywood bowl below shows how dramatic such changes can be. It is a section that was cut from the base of a cherry tree when it was felled. Note the deep colour of the heartwood in contrast to the sapwood. Without encouragement, within three months, the flat disc had formed a natural bowl shape. In this case, the result was turned to advantage, but such deformation would create havoc in a worked piece of furniture.

*Right* A cherrywood bowl. Note the contrast between heartwood and sapwood.

*Below* An air-dried timber (lumber) stack.

## Air drying

Outdoors, timber will dry naturally to a certain extent. It must be stacked carefully to allow good ventilation. When treating hardwood, a sawmill will air dry the converted timber for a period of up to two years before further processing. The stack should be protected from the elements, and the layers separated by small sticks to encourage an even rate of drying and to reduce distortion. Some pale species of timber, such as sycamore, are prone to staining when very green, particularly where the sticks are laid. Initially, these may be *end-reared*, or stacked on end, to avoid this.

## Stability and movement

Shrinkage describes the behaviour of timber as it dries, whereas *movement* is the tendency of wood to expand or shrink after it has been seasoned depending on its surroundings. Wood species with high stability are less likely to deform if the rates of tangential and radial movement are similar.

Certain species of wood, such as Douglas fir, teak, iroko and yellow pine behave much better than others and are preferable if this is an important consideration when choosing your wood.

| Wood species with low movement and good stability | |
|---|---|
| **Softwoods** | **Hardwoods** |
| Western red cedar | Muninga |
| Douglas fir | Teak |
| European spruce | Mahogany |
| Yellow pine | South American cedar |
| Western hemlock | Iroko |

## Kiln drying

Air drying is a lengthy process and can be unpredictable, as it is subject to varying weather conditions and seasonal changes. Kiln drying allows quicker production, while the quality and performance of the timber can be improved by careful control of the drying conditions. Today, nearly all commercially available timber is kiln dried, apart from beams of large section. Softwoods are normally kiln dried immediately after conversion, any preservative treatment also being applied at this stage. After drying, the timber may be cut into smaller sizes for distribution; it is in this condition that it usually reaches the home woodworker. Timber will produce disappointing results if it is worked before the seasoning process is over.

## Moisture content

The moisture content of wood is measured as the percentage of its dry weight. A sample of fresh-sawn softwood weighing 10kg (22lb) might contain as much as 5kg (11lb) of water

### Moisture content

WATER EVAPORATION
4kg (9lb)

10kg (22lb)
GREEN TIMBER
(LUMBER)

+

6kg (13lb)
AIR-DRIED TIMBER

5½kg (12lb)
KILN-DRIED TIMBER

100% moisture
content

20% moisture
content

10% moisture
content

and the same amount of dry wood. It would be described as having 100 per cent moisture content. In practice, wood is never dried completely to a zero per cent moisture content, but eventually it will reach a level consistent with its environment, which is called the *equilibrium moisture content* (emc). This can range from 18 to 20 per cent outdoors down to as low as 8 or 9 per cent in a warm, dry atmosphere. Kiln-dried timber is usually produced at a level of 10 to 12 per cent moisture content. It is essential to understand how changes in

the emc can affect the performance of a finished piece of woodwork, as the wood continues to absorb and lose moisture in response to changing levels of temperature and humidity. This is why doors and windows tend to stick during the cold months. A cabinet door that fits perfectly in the workshop can shrink or distort when installed in an air-conditioned, heated house. Consider storing the timber where it is to be used to allow it to acclimatize before being worked.

Moisture content can be estimated using a moisture meter. The meter must be suitably calibrated for the species concerned, and it will give only local values for moisture content, which will vary through the thickness of the wood. It provides a guide when monitoring timber as it dries.

### Drying defects

As wood dries, it shrinks, and distortion can occur in the finished boards, partly because the shrinkage will be uneven. This is predictable to an extent, depending on how it is converted. It moves more readily in the direction of the growth rings, and a plain-sawn board can lose as much as ten per cent of its original width in drying. Quarter-sawn boards are more stable, and are often used for wide areas of panelling for this reason. Uneven grain and tensions within the timber can result in defects in a board as it dries, or when it is worked. Here are some of the common problems:

Cupping on a
plain-sawn board

Less distortion
on a quarter-
sawn board

Bow

Spring

Twist or
wind

*Above* Wood stacked high in a kiln.

# SELECTING AND STORING WOOD

**There are so many different species of timber (lumber) that it may seem difficult to decide where to start when making a selection. Your choice will depend on a number of factors, not least the cost and availability. It is well worth tracking down one or more suppliers who understand the needs of woodworkers, and striking up a good working relationship with them.**

### Choosing

Many stockists are set up to provide for the construction trade and do not take kindly to requests for small quantities of less common types. On the other hand, sometimes bargains are to be had from such companies, when they are left with short lengths of wood (sometimes sold as shorts or short ends) that are less useful to the trade. Also, bear in mind that boards with constructional defects, areas of sapwood or wild, knotty grain can be used to good decorative effect if selected carefully.

Although certain species of timber are specified for many of the projects in this book, the information should be used as a guide. Quite often, the first stage in the process of deciding what to make is to consider what timber is available and how its potential can be realized to the full, rather than sticking to fixed ideas. It is very rare that a substitute wood cannot be found that possesses the desired properties.

*Right* Stacking wood the correct way in a timber (lumber) yard.

### Workability

Some timbers are noted for being easily worked, with a low cutting resistance and blunting effect on tools. They tend to be quite bland in appearance, but are ideal for making solid frameworks where accurate jointing and stability are important. Straight, even grain gives good glued joints and resistance to splitting when nailed or screwed. These timbers can be obtained at relatively low cost.

### Finish

Not all species of timber will take a good finish – if the grain is very coarse, the surface can "pick up", requiring a lengthy process of filling the grain and rubbing down to produce a satisfactory result. Some species, such as teak, have a natural oily content that inhibits the bonding of the finish. Over the years, some woods have become highly prized for their lustrous qualities and their ability to take a high polish. Naturally they tend to be more expensive and hard to obtain.

## Wood species with good working properties

Agba
Alder
Basswood
Obeche
Pine (most species)
Western red cedar

*Left* American basswood, or American lime, is fine grained, and easily worked without blunting your tools.

## Wood species with good finishing qualities

Afrormosia
Ash
Cherry
Hemlock
Jarrah
Mahogany
Rosewood
Walnut

*Left* American black walnut, with its marked grain figure, is popular for high-quality cabinet-making and carving. It polishes to an excellent finish.

## Durability

Timber (lumber) should be selected for durability if it will be exposed to moisture, not only outdoors, but also in areas of high humidity or condensation, such as kitchens and bathrooms. Sapwood is perishable and prone to staining in most timbers, but even the heartwood of some species is vulnerable. Many tropical hardwoods, and softwoods such as yew and cedar, are highly resistant to rot because of their oily nature.

## Density

The density of wood (expressed as kilograms per cubic metre or pounds per cubic foot) is not only a measure of its relative weight, but is also linked to its strength and durability. Where these are important, your choice of species should reflect this. Bear in mind that most figures quoted are based on averages at a fixed moisture content, and the density of a single piece of wood can vary depending on its origin and growth conditions.

## Storing

Many woodworkers will hoard timber (lumber). A piece of prime quality will be set aside until the right job comes along, or because it is "too good to use". There is nothing wrong with this, provided you have the space: the timber will come to no harm if stored in the correct manner and conditions, and may even improve with age. Do not let this hoarding instinct get out of control and keep track of your stock and manage it sensibly. Record the origin and date of purchase of each batch, and do not mix them in the same piece of work.

If you do not have enough space to keep all your stock in the workshop, it will survive perfectly well outdoors until it is needed. Bring it indoors well before working it though, to allow it to acclimatize to interior conditions.

### Common durable wood species in order of durability

| Less durable | Very durable |
|---|---|
| Alder | Teak |
| Birch | Iroko |
| Lime | Afrormosia |
| Ash | Jarrah |
| Poplar | Chestnut |
| Spruce | Oak |
| | Cedar |

*Above right* Cedar of Lebanon (a true cedar), has a high resin content, and it is light and durable, one of the few softwoods suitable for exterior use without preservative treatment.

### Common wood species in order of density

| Softwood | Temperate hardwoods | Tropical hardwoods |
|---|---|---|
| Western red cedar *(least dense)* | Basswood *(least dense)* | Obeche *(least dense)* |
| Spruce | Poplar | Agba |
| Hemlock | Alder | Meranti, Idigbo |
| Scots pine | Sycamore, Ash | Mahogany, Abura |
| Douglas fir | Elm, Chestnut | Iroko, Muninga |
| Larch | Walnut, Cherry | Utile, Sapele |
| Parana pine | Beech, Birch | Teak |
| Pitch pine | Oak, Rock maple | Afrormosia |
| Yew *(most dense)* | Jarrah *(most dense)* | Ebony *(most dense)* |

Plywood cover sheet

Overlap

Sticks

Bearers

**How to construct a storage stack**

Store long lengths of timber under cover, and ensure good ventilation. Warm, damp conditions encourage decay, and an attack of fungus in a wood store must be avoided at all costs. The spores that spread fungi are everywhere, and all they need are the right conditions to take hold.

# BUYING WOOD

Over a quarter of the land area of the globe is occupied by forested regions, and we reduce it at our peril. Unlike many other materials that we consume, trees are a renewable resource – it makes no sense to ignore the potential for endless supply by not replacing them as we use them. Gradually, the timber (lumber) trade is becoming aware of this, and the responsible woodworker should encourage the attitude by seeking out suppliers who operate environmentally sound purchasing policies.

### Timber awareness

There are organizations such as the Forestry Stewardship Council (FSC) and the American Forest and Paper Association (AF&PA) that are working worldwide to encourage certification schemes that promote the sustainable management of our forests.

Seek out the sources of timber available to you and satisfy yourself that your local supplier is aware of the issues involved.

### The timber trade

The trade market has a great responsibility, not only in forestry management and purchasing policy, but in promoting the efficient use of the raw material. Poor-quality timber can be directed toward the mass needs of industry while the best is reserved for the most demanding use. Everyone in the chain of supply, from foresters down to individual woodworkers, has a part to play in grading and selecting the correct timber for its purpose. When

*Above* For a wood-product manufacturer, the use of wood from FSC sources shows a commitment to the conservation of the world's forests.

specifying and buying timber, be prepared to consider alternatives to avoid wasting a valuable resource. Already some species are endangered and no longer available commercially, such as Brazilian rosewood; others are in short supply or are best converted into veneers. There is nothing wrong with using sheet materials, manufactured from timber trimmings (wood scraps) too small to use as solid wood, to provide a stable base for veneered panels or to make the components that will not be seen in a finished piece of work.

There are real cost savings to be made, too, if timber of the correct size and quality is purchased. Buying timber that has been dimensioned, or re-sawn to a predetermined size, saves handling large boards if you do not have the facilities. If timber has been *prepared*, or planed all round with square edges and smooth faces, it is ready to use without further machining. Bear in mind that each stage of the preparation process adds more cost. In the long term, it may pay you to invest in the space and equipment to machine your own stock from rough-sawn boards, allowing you to use the stock more selectively.

### Identifying timber

The timber trade has its own terminology for describing the different grades and appearance of the product. Some of the more common terms are specified in the accompanying panel; look out for them when specifying timber. There is a comprehensive range of common

*Above* The country of origin of imported product is identified by distinctive shipping marks on the wood.

timbers suitable for practical woodworking. One of the first hazards to be aware of when selecting timber is that the common name for each species can be a pitfall. Many species are known by various names in different parts of the world, or even in the same country; just as often, the same name can be applied to more than one species.

The system of naming timbers is not deliberately intended to confuse, although it does seem that way sometimes. It came about because suppliers from different countries used their own systems of timber identification to suit their own market, sometimes for convenience, and even, it must be said, to give their product more value. "Mahogany", for example, is used to describe completely different species of timber from South and Central America, Africa, and Australia. "Douglas fir" is not a true fir, and although it is also known as "Oregon pine", it is not a true pine either. You have every right to be confused!

The best way through the maze is to refer to the botanical name of a species, which is unique to each one, and should always be checked with the supplier when specifying the product you wish to buy. The first half of the name describes the genus or botanical group; the second part is the particular species within that group.

*Above* Douglas fir, or Oregon pine, is a softwood with a distinguishing grain.

## Timber trade terminology

| | |
|---|---|
| **Rough-sawn** | Sawn on a bandmill or circular saw to approximate dimensions. |
| **Prepared** | Planed in a sawmill. |
| **Surfaced** | Only small areas of a board are planed to give the buyer an idea of the colour or grain figure of the timber. |
| **PAR** | Prepared all round: square-section timber with machined faces. Beware: exact finished sizes will vary (see below). |
| **Nominal size** | The original size of the stock before machining: "ex 50 x 100mm" ("ex 2 x 4in") describes the nominal size. |
| **Finished size** | The true size of prepared stock after machining. Approximately 3mm (⅛in) will be removed from each face during this process. |
| **A/D** | Air-dried timber. Expect it to be no less than 18% moisture content. |
| **K/D** | Kiln dried. Usually timber is dried in the kiln to around 12% moisture content. |
| **T/T** | Through and through. Boards converted by through-and-through cutting will be plain sawn. |
| **1/SE** | One square edge. Boards with one square edge and one waney (crooked) edge, likely to be rift sawn. |
| **Waney edge** | Board with the sapwood and uneven edge still present, although the bark will have been removed. |
| **Unsorted** | Surprisingly, this describes the best grade for joinery-quality softwoods. Also termed clears, or clear and better. |
| **4ths & 5ths** | Lower-grade softwood stock. |
| **FAS** | Firsts and seconds. The best grade to look for in hardwoods graded for good-quality work. At least 83% of each board will yield clear, defect-free usable timber in large sizes. |
| **Commons** | Second-grade hardwood, yielding between 67 and 83% clear timber in smaller lengths. Acceptable for cabinet-making and small projects. |

## Timber and the environment

Forests Forever is encouraging companies to adopt an Environmental Timber Purchasing Policy. Companies are encouraged to set environmental objectives and targets, and to internally audit their progress towards these targets. In particular, they are encouraged to implement a programme to assess and monitor the environmental and legal credentials of all their timber products suppliers, and to trace timber as far as possible to the forest of origin.

While you shouldn't boycott individual species, it is possible to play a positive environmental role by seeking to specify a wider range of timber species. The use of "lesser-known species" can assist certain countries, usually in the tropics, with the implementation of their national sustainability programmes by taking pressure off those species which have, in the past, formed the mainstream of business. With a larger number of commercially valuable tree species, forestry departments have greater flexibility in planning harvesting regimes to ensure a better species balance in the future.

Bear in mind that in seeking to increase the range of species used, you shouldn't compromise on quality or performance. Your choice of species should always be governed by the need to ensure that it is technically suited to the application. However, keep an open mind to alternatives and don't be put off simply because a species name is unfamiliar.

# SOFTWOODS

This type of wood is not necessarily soft, but all softwoods have in common the property of being conifers, or cone-bearing trees, and mostly evergreen, although the larch is a notable exception. Usually low in cost and readily available, most common softwoods are suitable for all forms of general carcassing and construction work.

If better appearance and good finishing qualities are required, more careful selection is necessary. Softwoods are generally light in weight, less durable, and more susceptible to insect attack and fungal decay than most hardwoods. Pitch pine, cedar and yew are three notable exceptions.

*Opposite left, centre and right*
The storage chest is made from reclaimed pine floorboards; the magazine rack is pine; and the bar stool is constructed from Southern yellow pine.

| | Common name | Other names | Botanical name | Origin |
|---|---|---|---|---|
| Cedar of Lebanon | Cedar of Lebanon | True cedar | *Cedrus libani* | Middle East, Europe |
| | Douglas fir | Oregon pine | *Pseudotsuga taxifolia* | USA, Canada |
| | Hoop pine | Queensland pine | *Araucaria cunninghamii* | Australia |
| | Kauri pine | Queensland kauri | *Agathis* spp. | Australia, NZ |
| | Larch | European larch | *Larix decidua* | Europe, Asia |
| | Parana pine | | *Araucaria angustifolia* | S America |
| | Pitch pine | Longleaf pitch pine | *Pinus palustris* | USA, Central America |
| | Ponderosa pine | Bull pine | *Pinus ponderosa* | USA, Canada |
| | Rimu | Red pine | *Dacrydium cupressinum* | New Zealand |
| | Scots pine | European redwood | *Pinus sylvestris* | UK, Europe |
| | Sequoia | Californian redwood | *Sequoia sempervirens* | USA |
| Larch | Silver fir | European whitewood | *Abies alba* | Europe |
| | Southern yellow pine | Carolina pine | *Pinus echinata, Pinus eliottii* | USA |
| | Spruce | European whitewood | *Picea excelsa, Picea abies* | Europe |
| | Western hemlock | Alaska pine | *Tsuga heterophylla* | USA, Canada |
| | Western red cedar | Shinglewood | *Thuja plicata* | USA, Canada |
| | Yellow pine | Quebec yellow pine | *Pinus strobus* | USA, Canada |
| Southern yellow pine | Yew | | *Taxus baccata* | UK, Europe |

Yellow pine

| Description | Other properties | |
|---|---|---|
| Light brown heartwood, with distinctive growth rings | Very resinous, durable, easy to work, but low in strength | |
| Yellow to pinkish brown with marked growth rings | Slightly coarse, quite dense, durable with good workability | |
| Yellow brown heartwood, pale sapwood, as Parana pine | Not a true pine. Works and finishes well, very stable | |
| Fine, straight grained, creamy brown colour | Again not a true pine, but works well and is durable | |
| Resinous with pale sapwood and reddish heart | Heavier and more durable, but harder to work | |
| Attractive reddish brown heartwood with dark streaks | Straight grained and good workability, but poor stability |  |
| Marked figure with yellowish to reddish heartwood | Coarse grained and resinous, but very durable | Douglas fir |
| Yellowish white, straight grained with delicate figure | Very stable, works well, excellent finishing | |
| Reddish brown heartwood with fine texture | Not a true pine, but equivalent working properties | |
| Pink to reddish heartwood with distinct growth rings | Resinous, good all-round working and performance | |
| Prominent growth rings, reddish brown heartwood | Similar to Western red cedar, but non-resinous | |
| Very similar to Spruce, sold generally as Whitewood | Soft and lightweight especially when fast grown |  |
| Yellow to reddish brown heart with marked growth rings | More durable and stable than Yellow pine | Scots pine |
| Pale white with sapwood and heartwood very similar | Can be knotty and contain pockets of resin | |
| Fine, straight grain with dark red growth rings | Good workability and finish, but prone to movement | |
| Attractive heartwood varies from light pink to dark brown | Very stable and durable, but soft and low in strength | |
| Light tan to pinkish heartwood, good even texture | Good quality, stable, and slightly resinous |  |
| Pale sapwood and reddish heart with colourful figure | Dense, oily wood works to a fine finish | Western hemlock |

Yew

# TEMPERATE HARDWOODS

There are thousands of species of hardwood to choose from, but those listed here have been selected because of their ready availability, cost and performance. Temperate hardwoods are grown away from the tropical belt, in Europe, Asia, North America and the Southern Hemisphere. They offer a vast range of different properties, making it possible to find a particular species to suit virtually any purpose.

*Opposite left, centre and right*
The occasional table is constructed from white ash; the picture frame from white oak; and the settle from sweet chestnut.

| | Common name | Other names | Botanical name | Origin |
|---|---|---|---|---|
| Alder (American) | Alder (American) | Red alder | *Alnus rubra* | USA |
| | Ash | European ash | *Fraxinus excelsior* | USA, Europe |
| | Australian blackwood | | *Acacia melanoxylon* | Australia |
| Basswood | Basswood | American lime | *Tilia americana* | USA, Canada |
| | Beech | | *Fagus sylvatica* | Europe, Asia |
| | Birch (European) | White birch | *Betula alba* | Europe, Asia |
| | Boxwood | | *Buxus sempervirens* | Europe |
| Birch (European) | Butternut | White walnut | *Juglans cinerea* | USA |
| | Cherry | American cherry | *Prunus serotina* | USA |
| | Chestnut | Sweet chestnut | *Castanea sativa* | UK, Europe |
| Chestnut | Elm (European) | English elm | *Ulmus procera* | Europe |
| | Hornbeam | | *Carpinus betulus* | UK, Europe |
| | Jarrah | Australian mahogany | *Eucalyptus marginata* | Australia |
| | Maple (Hard) | Sugar maple | *Acer saccharum* | USA, Canada |
| Jarrah | Maple (Soft) | Red maple | *Acer rubrum* | USA, Canada |
| | Oak (American Red) | | *Quercus rubra* | USA |
| | Oak (American White) | | *Quercus alba* | USA |
| Oak (European) | Oak (European) | | *Quercus robur* | Europe |
| | Sycamore (American) | Buttonwood, Lacewood | *Platanus occidentalis* | USA |
| | Sycamore (European) | | *Acer pseudoplatanus* | Europe |
| | Walnut (Australian) | Queensland walnut | *Endiandra palmerstonii* | Australia |
| Sycamore (American) | Walnut (Black) | Virginia walnut | *Juglans nigra* | USA |
| | Walnut (European) | | *Juglans regia* | Europe |
| | Yellow poplar | American whitewood | *Liriodendron tulipifera* | USA |

| Description | Other properties | |
|---|---|---|
| Light brown, fine straight grain | Works well, but non-durable | |
| Pale honey colour with marked growth ring figure | Good working and bending properties, excellent finish | |
| Gold or red to dark brown with sometimes curly figure | Strong, works well and polishes to a high finish | |
| Creamy white with close even grain | Low in strength and durability, works and carves very well | Ash |
| Pale brown with distinctive flecks | Hard, but good to work and finish | |
| White or pale brown with little figure | Soft and easy to work | |
| Pale yellow brown, fine even grain | Very dense and hard, good carving and turning wood | |
| Light brown, straight coarse grain | Easily worked and very stable | Beech |
| Reddish brown with pale sapwood | Hard-wearing, but tough to work | |
| Light brown, similar to oak, but without silvery ray figure | Bends well, easy to work and reasonably durable | |
| Brown heartwood with twisted grain | Attractive, but hard to work | |
| Uniform close grain, yellowish white | Very hard-wearing, but hard to work | Cherry |
| Rich red heartwood, wavy figure | Strong, durable, but low in stability | |
| Very close grain, creamy brown | Dense and hard wood, polishes well | |
| Pinkish tinge to heartwood | Softer and lighter than above | Elm (European) |
| Pinkish brown compared to *Q. robur* | Less obvious ray figure | |
| Lighter, but similar to *Q. robur* | Less durable than European oak | |
| Pale to dark brown; distinct growth rings and silvery rays | Strong and durable, bends well, harder to work | |
| Light brown, straight even grain with wide rays | Ray figure produces attractive "lacewood" when rift sawn | Maple (hard) |
| Very pale, sometimes wavy grain | Stains and finishes well | |
| Similar to European walnut | Interlocking grain, harder to work | |
| Dark brown with purple tints | Coarse grain, but good to work | Oak (American red) |
| Greyish brown with rich dark streaks and wavy grain | Excellent finish, hard and durable | |
| Pale sapwood, dark streaks in heartwood, straight grain | Good working properties and good finishing, stable | |

Walnut (black)

# TROPICAL HARDWOODS

Tropical hardwoods have become a sensitive issue in recent times, as large areas of tropical rainforest around the world have been cleared by indiscriminate logging. This is not to say that some sources of tropical timber (lumber) are not managed responsibly. Indeed, where they are, they should be encouraged as a means of supporting local industries in the sustainable management of the resource. Identifying the species at risk (see chart) and using alternatives with similar properties is a responsible approach to the problem.

*Opposite left and right* The legs of the dining table are constructed from teak and the top is from elm. The conservatory bench is made from iroko.

| | Common name | Other names | Botanical name | Origin |
|---|---|---|---|---|
| Afrormosia | Afrormosia | | *Pericopsis elata* | W Africa |
| | Balsawood | | *Ochroma lagopus* | S America |
| | Brazilian cedar | | *Cedrela fissilis* | S America |
| | ● Bubinga | African rosewood | *Guibourtia demeusei* | W Africa |
| Bubinga | ● Cocobolo | Nicaragua rosewood | *Dalbergia retusa* | Central America |
| | ● Ebony | Macassar ebony | *Diospyros macassar* | Indonesia |
| | Greenheart | | *Ocotea rodiaei* | S America |
| | Idigbo | | *Terminalia ivorensis* | W Africa |
| Idigbo | Iroko | African teak | *Chlorophora excelsa* | Central Africa |
| | Jelutong | | *Dyera costulata* | Indonesia |
| | ● Kingwood | Violetwood | *Dalbergia cearensis* | S America |
| | ● Lignum vitae | Ironwood | *Guaiacum officinale* | C & S America |
| Iroko | Mahogany (African) | | *Khaya ivorensis* | W Africa |
| | ● Mahogany (Brazilian) | | *Swietenia macrophylla* | C & S America |
| | Makore | African cherry | *Tieghemella heckelii* | W Africa |
| | Meranti | Lauan, Seraya | *Shorea* spp. | Indonesia, Philippines |
| Makore | Obeche | African whitewood | *Triplochiton scleroxylon* | W Africa |
| | Padauk | African or Indian padauk | *Pterocarpus* spp. | SE Asia, W Africa |
| | Ramin | Melawis | *Gonystylus macrophyllum* | Indonesia |
| | ● Rosewood (Brazilian) | Rio rosewood, Jacaranda | *Dalbergia negra* | S America |
| Meranti | ● Rosewood (Indian) | | *Dalbergia latifolia* | India |
| | Sapele | | *Entandophragma cylindricum* | W Africa |
| | ● Satinwood | | *Chloroxylon swietenia* | India, Sri Lanka |
| | ● Teak | | *Tectona grandis* | SE Asia |
| | Utile | | *Entandrophragma utile* | W Africa |
| Teak | Wenge | | *Milletia laurentii* | W Africa |

● *Endangered species*

| Description | Other properties | |
|---|---|---|
| Orange-brown, straight and fine-textured heartwood | Stable and durable, good alternative to teak and less oily |  |
| Pale beige, porous and open-grained | Lightest and softest of all hardwoods | |
| Pink to mahogany coloured heartwood | Durable and good to work, resinous | |
| Reddish brown with dark figure | Hard and dense, coarse grained | Brazilian cedar |
| Dark brown with colourful streaks | Tough and dense with lustrous finish | |
| Dark brown with black stripes | Dense, used for turning and veneers in small quantities | |
| Yellowish to dark olive brown | Extremely durable, hard to work | |
| Pale yellowish with some figure | Stable and durable, poor finishing | Ebony |
| Yellowish to golden brown, with coarse striped grain | Durable with lustrous finish; hard to work and blunts tools | |
| Straight grained, pale creamy colour | Lightweight and stable, works well | |
| Even-textured with variegated figure from brown to violet | Lustrous and excellent finish, used for turning or veneers | |
| Olive to deep brown, interlocked grain and fine texture | Oily, hard and extremely dense, used mainly for turning | Mahogany (Brazilian) |
| Pale pinkish brown, with coarse or interlocking grain | Easy to work, reasonable substitute for true mahogany | |
| Light to dark reddish brown, straight and even grain | Stable with excellent working properties, good finishing | |
| Reddish brown, fine straight grain | Hard, dense and difficult to work | Obeche |
| Pink (White lauan) or reddish (Red lauan), coarse grain | Easy to work, often seen as Far Eastern plywood | |
| Creamy white to yellow, open grained | Light, but stable, easily worked | |
| Red to purplish brown; resinous and interlocking grain | Hard-wearing, very stable, hard to work and poor finish | |
| Straw to creamy brown with dark flecks, straight grained | Easy working, but poor stability, often used for mouldings | Ramin |
| Dark brown with variegated violet to dark bronze streaks | Attractive, but in short supply, used mainly for veneering | |
| More dull brown to purplish black | As for Brazilian rosewood | |
| Reddish brown; markedly striped quartered figure | Alternative to mahogany, easy to work, but less stable | Rosewood (Brazilian) |
| Golden brown with lustrous figure | Good to work, hard fine texture | |
| Honey coloured to dark brown with strong figure | Dense, oily, durable, attractive but hard to work | |
| Reddish brown, interlocking grain | Similar to sapele, but more stable | |
| Dark brown with black stripes | Hard and dense, attractive finish | Sapele |

# MANUFACTURED BOARDS

Manufactured boards in various forms are familiar and have revolutionized the principles of wooden construction. By processing solid timber (lumber) into sheets of stable material, glued together by various means, the suppliers have considerably increased their usable output and have improved the material's performance for many uses. Parts of the tree that otherwise would be pulped can be reformed to produce an economic building material. For the woodworker, the main advantage is the availability of large panels that are stable, easy to work and low in cost.

### Plywood

This consists of several thin layers of wood, usually with the grain at right angles in alternate layers (cross-ply). It is dimensionally stable and very strong. Useful thicknesses range from 3mm (⅛in) up to 25mm (1in).

*Softwood ply* is usually made from Douglas fir, and is coarse grained, but durable.

*Birch ply* has more laminations and is pre-sanded to give a smooth finish that is ideal for painting or varnishing.

*Far Eastern ply* is cheaper, but more open grained and more useful for structural work.

*Exterior-grade ply* uses a WBP (water- and boil-proof) adhesive and hardwood laminations.

*Marine ply* is the most durable of all and correspondingly expensive.

*Flexiply* has the grain running in the same direction on every layer and can be formed into tight curves. It also has no "voids" in its structure.

*Decorative ply* has a veneer of decorative hardwood bonded to one or both sides and is perfect for enclosed panels and carcass construction.

### Blockboard

The core of blockboard is made from solid strips of softwood glued along their edges. It is faced with a layer of veneer on each side. Blockboard is lighter than plywood, resistant to bending, and is useful for large structures and shelving. Normally, it is available only in 19mm (¾in) and 25mm (1in) thicknesses.

### Laminboard

Similar to blockboard, laminboard has an internal core made of much smaller strips of softwood. As a result, the board is more stable. It is ideal for a smooth, ripple-free finish.

### Particle boards

In particle boards, no thin layers of solid wood are used at all. Instead, the board is made from small particles of processed timber bonded together with resin.

*Above* MDF is stable and easy to work, and ideal for making templates in the workshop.

*Chipboard* is the most common type, being used as a base for laminated work or for utility shelving and carcassing. It has a smooth, hard surface and a softer core. Unlike plywood, it is prone to splitting when screws are driven into the edges.

*OSB* (oriented strand board) is similar to chipboard, but is made from larger, wafer-like particles and has uneven faces. Both types can be used to provide hard-wearing surfaces for bench tops and flooring, but they have poor moisture resistance and low integral strength. Chipboard shelving is prone to sagging unless well supported at close intervals.

*Pineboard* is like the core of blockboard, but without the outer layers. Small strips of pine are glued together on edge and sanded smooth,

Marine ply 6mm (¼in)

Far Eastern 5-ply 12mm (½in)

Hardboard

Chipboard

12mm (½in) medium-density fibreboard

19mm (¾in) medium-density fibreboard

Blockboard

Pineboard

making it ideal for instant shelving, carcassing and many home improvement projects.

## Fibreboards

Wood is shredded into a fibrous form and bonded with resin under high pressure to manufacture various forms of fibreboard.

*Softboard* or *Insulating board* is extremely light and soft. It can be used as an insulating layer or as a pinboard.

*Hardboard* has one hard surface only, but is very stable and bends easily. It is useful for making templates.

*Tempered hardboard* is impregnated with resins to make it more water-resistant, but by no means is it completely waterproof.

*MDF* (medium-density fibreboard) is by far the most useful fibreboard product. It is dense, flat, stiff, has no knots and is easy to cut. It is very stable, and the fibres are compressed so finely that it can be cut and shaped without crumbling. It is best cut with carbide tools as steel cutting tools may dull easily. MDF makes an ideal substrate for veneer, and is available in decorative form with real hardwood veneers already bonded to both faces. Always wear a mask when working with MDF, as it creates fine dust particles which can be carcinogenic. Glues for MDF are also made with formaldehyde and are toxic.

## Standard sizes

Nearly all manufactured boards have a standard size of 1220 x 2440mm (4 x 8ft). Some suppliers offer a metric size, which is smaller (1200 x 2400mm), so always check, as this can make a critical difference to your cutting list. Special sizes of plywood and MDF, up

*Right* An indication of the wide range of finishes that manufactured boards can offer.

to 3m (10ft) in length, are available from some suppliers. Many stores will cut large sheets into smaller sizes if requested at the time of purchase.

## Grain direction

The direction in which the grain runs on the outer layers is always given first when describing plywood. This can be important when planning your cutting

list. With birch plywood, for example, 1220 x 2440mm (4 x 8ft) in a supplier's catalogue will indicate that the grain runs across the width of the board, not down its length.

Most veneered decorative boards are manufactured with the grain running across the length. In this case, the catalogue entry would read 2440 x 1220mm (8 x 4ft).

### Common thicknesses of manufactured board

| Type | 3mm 1/8in | 6mm 1/4in | 9mm 3/8in | 12mm 1/2in | 16mm 5/8in | 19mm 3/4in | 22mm 7/8in | 25mm 1in | 32mm 1¼in |
|---|---|---|---|---|---|---|---|---|---|
| Plywood | X | X | X | X | X | X | X | X | |
| Plywood (D. fir) | | | | X | | X | | | |
| Blockboard | | | | | | X | | X | |
| Laminboard | | | | | | X | | X | |
| Chipboard | | | | X | X | X | X | X | |
| OSB | | | | X | | X | | | |
| Hardboard | X | X | | | | | | | |
| MDF | | X | X | X | | X | | X | X |

# TOOLS

**W**oodworking requires a range of specific tools, which have been developed and become increasingly specialized to suit every conceivable task. Despite the introduction of power tools in recent years, few jobs can be done without using hand tools at some stage of the process, and every woodworker will gradually collect more of them as the need arises. The following pages include most of the tools in common use, but there is no end to the variety and different levels of quality and refinement available, as browsing through any tool catalogue will reveal.

Tools can be grouped into families according to each stage of the woodworking process – measuring and marking, cutting and shaping and finishing, for example. Only a few basic essentials from each group are needed to begin, but the serious craftsperson will soon find that learning new skills and acquiring the tools that go with them is a never-ending process, and part of the rewarding experience of fine woodworking.

# THE BASIC TOOLKIT

"A bad craftsman always blames his tools." We have all heard this saying and understand what it means – you cannot expect a tool to do its job well if it is not handled correctly. This does not simply mean that you need to develop your woodworking skills; you also have to select the appropriate tool for the task at hand, understand how it functions and know how to keep it sharp and in good condition.

It will take some time and a little patience to gain confidence using hand tools, especially saws, chisels and planes but you will gain much satisfaction and increase your skills as a craftsperson.

### Buying the best

A common mistake made by novices is to start out with a cheap "beginner's" toolkit. This can be false economy – not only will the tools be made of poor-quality steel that will not hold a sharp edge, but also their overall quality and balance will make hard work of simple operations. As a result, you may become frustrated at your inability to achieve good results, no matter how much care you take, and lose interest in persevering.

There must be many people who think that they do not have what it takes for woodworking, when in fact all they need is the correct guidance and a little tuition in selecting the tools for the job.

*Below* Build your tool collection gradually by buying the best tools you can afford.

## Starting a collection

| | Basic toolkit | Next on the list |
|---|---|---|
| Measuring and marking: | Retractable tape<br>Try square<br>Marking knife<br>Bradawl or awl | Steel rule<br>Combination square<br>Marking gauge<br>Adjustable bevel gauge |
| Cutting: | Hardpoint saw<br>Tenon saw | Professional hand saw<br>Mitre saw |
| Shaping: | Bench plane<br>Bevelled chisels | Block plane<br>Firmer chisels |
| Assembling: | Screwdrivers<br>Claw hammer<br>Mallet<br>G-clamps | Cordless drill/driver<br>Drill bits<br>Pin hammer<br>Sash (bar) clamps |
| Finishing: | Sandpaper/abrasive papers | Scraper |

### Getting the essentials

It is not easy to specify the tools that are essential for starting out, simply because the range of woodworking activities is so wide. A model maker needs different tools to a cabinet-maker; working with manufactured boards requires sharp, tungsten-carbide-tipped tools for best results, while softwoods can be worked easily with good-quality hand tools.

Nevertheless, most woodworking operations tend to have a definite sequence of work, and the basics will allow you to get started and explore further options as you progress. Included in the table are the tools that should form your "wish list" – the most useful items to save for.

## Buying tools

Most large hardware and do-it-yourself stores stock a full range of tools and offer good value where the more basic items are concerned. For the best quality and a wider range of specialist (specialty) tools, however, a professional tool shop is worth a visit. An expensive hand saw or plane must be handled and tested for balance before you buy.

A good tool supplier will understand this and should be able to offer a variety of different models so that you can choose the one that suits you best.

Spare parts and servicing are important, so try to develop a good working relationship with your supplier and discuss your needs. Remember that many expensive tools can be hired (rented) rather than purchased outright, if you need them only for the occasional project. This is also a good way of trying out different makes and models before buying a tool for yourself.

Browsing through tool catalogues is another habit that most woodworkers share. You cannot handle the tools or try them out, but a good mail-order supplier will offer a very wide range and can be a good source for really specialized items. Even second-hand tool shops are worth visiting if you get the chance. Examine the tools carefully to check that they are not damaged or incomplete; you may find a real bargain. Old tool steel was forged to a high quality and is definitely superior to some of today's cheap varieties.

## Storing tools

Well-made tools are works of great craftsmanship in themselves. They should be chosen with care and looked after well. Most accomplished craftsmen still possess some of the first tools they ever acquired, even though

they may be many years old. Always protect the cutting edges of tools. A good-quality hand saw needs a cover that clips over the blade – you can make one from thin strips of plywood or plastic tube if one was not supplied with the saw. Keep chisels in a leather tool roll, with divisions to separate the blades. Planes should always have their blades retracted when not in use and be stored on their sides to preserve the surface of the sole plate.

When buying power tools, the more professional models will usually be supplied in a carrying case, which should be considered a necessity rather than a luxury. As well as protecting the tool from dust, it will prevent damage to the power lead (cord), and keep the accessories safe so that they are to hand when needed.

### Power tools

Portable power tools represent a greater investment than hand tools and must be chosen carefully. They are listed in order of versatility and usefulness.

- Jigsaw
- Cordless drill
- Router
- Orbital sander
- Circular saw
- Power drill
- Power plane (planer)
- Belt sander
- Biscuit jointer
- Mitre saw

*Below* A good set of chisels, with high-quality steel blades that are kept sharp, will last for many years.

# TOOLS FOR MEASURING AND MARKING

**Accurate marking out is always the first step to a successful job. Poor-quality measuring and marking devices can lose their accuracy very quickly and spoil your work without you realizing until it is too late. Check them regularly for wear and damage, and if you think an item is suspect, put it to one side or dispose of it. A common mistake is to keep such a tool as a spare, but this is a false economy. A try square, for example, should form a perfect 90 degree angle – any variation makes it useless.**

### Units of measurement

When buying measuring and marking instruments, always check which units are used on the scale. Even though metrication of the woodworking trade has been in progress for many years, there are no signs of the imperial system dying out and certainly not in the United States. Suppliers, toolmakers and timber (lumber) yards seem to manage to work to both systems in parallel, and woodworkers need to be able to do the same. It is not as confusing as it seems, but there is always room for misunderstanding. Double check the specifications of the tools when you buy them.

### Metric and imperial

A metric rule will be marked in millimetres or centimetres, or both; an imperial scale will be marked in feet and inches. Most useful of all might be a rule with both scales, on either side, but do remember to check that they are accurate. Some of the cheaper tools are poorly engraved or printed, and an inaccurate scale is not worth buying at any price.

**T-square** A combined straightedge and square for marking out.

**Straightedge** This is used as a measure and a guide for scoring and cutting. A large handle allows a firm grip and keeps fingers well away from the blade of a marking knife. A good straightedge will have thin friction pads on the underside to prevent it from slipping.

**Steel rule** For accurate setting out of joints and small dimensions, a steel rule with etched divisions is the best. It can be up to 1m or 36in long, but a 300mm (12in) rule will be more convenient for most marking-out tasks.

**Bench rule** (*below*) A long wooden rule, less accurate for fine detail, but suitable for bench joinery and general cabinet-making. Brass-tipped versions prevent damage to the ends.

**Mitre square** (*above*) This is not a "square" at all, but an accurately machined blade and stock set at 45 degrees for gauging perfectly mitred corners.

**Combination square** With a sliding scale and well-designed stock, this can be used as a try square, a mitre square and an adjustable depth gauge. This example even has a small spirit level mounted in the stock and a small pin for accurate marking.

**Adjustable bevel gauge or sliding bevel** The hardened steel blade with locking lever can be adjusted quickly for measuring and transferring angles. A rosewood stock with brass strips ensures lasting accuracy.

**Try square** The classic carpenter's square, with a rosewood stock and brass facings for consistent accuracy. One of the first items for your toolbox.

**Bradawl** This is similar to an awl, but with a small flat end to the blade. It is used for marking hole positions and can be twisted into the wood without splitting the grain.

**Craft knife** This has a multitude of uses, particularly for scribing and scoring the workpiece, as well as cutting. Choose a model with a retractable blade for safety.

**Retractable tape** An all-purpose measuring tape in a rigid case. Look for a good locking action, clear markings on the blade and a well-formed hooked end that allows both internal and external measurements.

**Spirit level** This is not vital for bench carpentry, but comes into its own when carrying out installation work. A small "torpedo" level can be kept in the toolbox.

**Chalk line** A quick method of marking out straight lines. Fill the reservoir with coloured chalk powder, clip the hook over one end of the work, pull the string tight and snap it lightly to leave a perfectly straight, temporary cutting line.

**Vernier gauge** Used for measuring both the inner and outer diameters of circular objects, or the widths of a mortise and tenon joint.

**Profile gauge** Small needles slide in the central stock, allowing the outline of any profile to be copied and transferred with ease.

**Mortise gauge** This is used to mark out consistently accurate, parallel lines for cutting a mortise. The two brass pins are independently adjustable on accurate brass slides, while the sliding stock runs against the face of the work. There is a single pin on the opposite side of the shaft for marking a single scribed line.

**Engineer's square** An all-metal square, precision made with a hardened blade. Ideal for checking detail and can be obtained with a blade as short as 75mm (3in).

**Awl** A small pointed blade for starting holes or pricking out a mark accurately.

# HAND SAWS

A well-balanced hand saw is an essential tool for any woodworker. Properly set and sharpened, it can produce a smooth, straight cut as quickly and even more accurately than a power saw. The performance of a saw depends on the size, shape and number of the teeth, which act as a series of miniature knives to slice through the wood. Each tooth is ground and sharpened individually, the quality of the steel determining how well it will perform.

**Crosscut saw** These are traditional saws. If they are well maintained, they will last a lifetime. Ideal specifications include a taper-ground blade, to prevent it from binding in the saw cut, with cross-ground teeth for splinter-free cutting across the grain. A 560mm (22in), 10- or 12-point saw is suitable for most tasks. A 10-point saw has ten tooth points for every 25mm (1in) of the blade.

**Hardpoint saw** Modern technology has produced saws with hardened teeth that remain sharp for longer, and have a specially ground profile for cutting along and across the grain with equal efficiency. However, hardpoint teeth cannot be resharpened.

**Utility saw** Consider using this "universal" saw for general-purpose use. It cannot be resharpened either, but can be considered as disposable when it has done its job. It is ideal for cutting manufactured materials, such as chipboard, which are less kind to traditional saws.

### Tenon saws

This family of saws (*below*) was designed for small-scale, accurate work, such as making joints and so on. The blade is stiffened with a strip of steel or brass along the back, and consequently these saws may be described as "backsaws". They have smaller teeth, typically 15-point, for a finer cut.

**Hardpoint tenon saw** Like the larger hand saw, this cannot be resharpened, but is ideal for general-purpose use.

**Dovetail saw** A smaller version for very fine joinery work, with 20-point teeth.

**Classic tenon saw** A good-quality tenon saw for the cabinet-maker.

## Special-purpose saws

Frame saws are designed for intricate work. The disposable blades are heat treated for hard wear and will cut wood, fibres or plastic. The frame allows the blade to be swivelled to any angle for cutting curves.

**Piercing saw** This has fine teeth (up to 80-point) for the finest modelling and engineering work. The quick-release facility allows the blade to be fed through the work and re-attached.

**Coping saw** Designed for quick adjustment, it allows curves to be cut by swivelling the blade within the frame.

**Fret saw** This can cut into the work as deep as 250mm (10in) from the edge before the frame impedes the cutting action. It works on the pull stroke for accurate control.

**Hardpoint padsaw** This has a short, stiff blade that allows small cut-outs to be made in panels where access is restricted. Hardpoint teeth will cut fibre- or plasterboard with ease.

**Pistol-grip padsaw** This allows greater control of the blade with a pistol grip. Interchangeable blades, including hacksaw blades, can be used for cutting thin sheet metal.

**Mitre box and mitre block** Useful sawing accessories without the expense of a mitre saw. To use them, insert a tenon saw blade into the pre-cut guide slots to make accurate square and mitre cuts. A mitre block has one slot, while a mitre box has two, to direct the saw blade.

**Mitre saw** This makes short work of cutting accurate angles and offers fine adjustment. It is well worth the investment if working with delicate mouldings or making picture frames. The hardpoint blade slides in nylon bearings, which, in turn, guide the cutting action.

Mitre box

Mitre block

# POWER SAWS

**Power saws can save a lot of time and hard work, but they can also do a lot of damage if used incorrectly. Never force a saw through the work. If the blade is not sharp, or the motor is underpowered, not only will the cut be inaccurate, but also you'll be putting your safety at risk. Let the saw do the work, guiding it slowly, but surely, along the line. Use an adjustable fence if possible when making straight parallel cuts.**

**Jigsaw** The all-purpose power saw with a multitude of uses. As well as making curved cuts, a jigsaw is ideal for quickly roughing-out work before finishing by hand.

Jigsaw

### Jigsaw key features:

- Pendulum action to reduce binding and increase the life of the blade.
- Variable speed for greater control to suit the thickness of material.
- A sawdust blower that directs the exhaust from the motor fan toward the cutting line to remove sawdust as you follow the line of the cut.
- An adjustable base plate to permit a variety of cutting angles.
- Scrolling action, allowing the blade itself to be swivelled for cutting curves of very small radius.

**Reciprocating or sabre saw** This is not really a common workshop tool, but it is useful for the rapid cutting of boards to length. Unless you do this frequently, a good, sharp hand saw will be just as effective.

Reciprocating saw

### Saw blades

Jigsaw blades come in a variety for many purposes, but check that the model of jigsaw you buy will accept standard-fitting blades. There are many specialized blades available for cutting all kinds of material, such as wood, manufactured boards, metal, ceramics, plastics and laminates. A knife blade has no teeth, and is designed for cutting leather or rubber sheeting.

Bi-metal blades, though more expensive, will last longer and are less inclined to bend. Most blades are 100mm (4in) long, allowing a depth of cut of 50–65mm (2–2½in), but heavy-duty blades are available up to 150mm (6in) long. These should only be fitted to a machine with a powerful motor designed to accept the extra load.

### Circular saw blades

Check that the bore of the blade (the diameter of the central hole that fits over the spindle) is compatible with the machine, as different makes vary. As with hand saws, the type of blade should suit the material and the cutting action, whether ripsawing along the grain, crosscutting, or making fine cuts in veneered or laminated panels.

Carbide teeth are cheaper for most general-purpose work; tungsten-carbide-tipped blades are sharper and much more hardwearing. They should be used when cutting composite materials and manufactured boards.

Powered mitre saws use special blades with teeth at a "negative rake" to suit the plunging action of the saw. They are not interchangeable with other machines.

Circular saw

**Circular saw** This is the best saw for cutting out large panels of plywood or similar manufactured materials. If it is used with a fence or purpose-made (custom-made) guide, it will make straight, smooth cuts with ease. The size of the machine and the diameter of blade determine the maximum depth of cut.

### Circular saw key features:

- Tungsten-carbide-tipped (TCT) blade.
- Adjustable base plate or "shoe" for depth and angle of cut.
- Sliding fence for cutting parallel to the edge of the work.
- Good visibility in front of the blade to aid control when cutting freehand.
- Spindle and also electric brakes to stop the blade spinning as soon as the trigger is released.
- Spindle lock for fitting blades quickly and safely.

Powered crosscut saw

**Powered crosscut saw** Sometimes called a mitre saw, this is a more costly item, but a useful workshop tool. It makes quick work of cross cutting timber (lumber) accurately to length with perfectly square ends, or can be adjusted to make angled cuts up to 45 degrees. The best models allow the saw body to slide out on parallel bars for cutting extra-wide stock up to 250mm (10in) and have a swivel mount for cutting compound angles.

**Cordless circular saw** This version of the circular saw comes into its own when working outdoors away from a power source. It does have the added safety advantage of not having a vulnerable power cord, and can be used one-handed for light work. Note how on the model shown, the blade is mounted on the left-hand side of the body for better visibility.

Cordless circular saw

# PLANES

Hand planes are among the most satisfying tools you can use. A finely set plane with a sharp blade will slice through the wood with an unmistakable sweet sound, leaving a smooth surface that scarcely needs any further treatment. As with other tools, different sizes and types of plane have been developed over the years to suit each particular task perfectly.

### Bench planes

This is the standard family of planes for two-handed use on the workbench. Each type is designed for a specific function, depending on the length of the body and the angle, or set, of the blade. Try planes or jointer planes have bodies of up to 600mm (24in) in length and are used for "trying", or truing-up (squaring), perfectly straight edges. Fore planes are slightly shorter, at 460mm (18in), and are used for much the same purpose as the try plane.

## Anatomy of a bench plane

The base of the plane is called the sole, or sole plate, and should be protected from damage to keep it perfectly straight and flat. The mouth in the sole allows the shavings to be cleared away as the plane is used. The frog is the machined block that receives the blade assembly; it can be adjusted to alter the width of the mouth. It is set to the ideal position during manufacture. Adjustment levers are mounted in the frog to control the depth of cut and to keep the blade perfectly straight. The blade assembly is removable for sharpening and maintenance, and consists of three parts: the blade itself, or plane iron, made of high-quality carbon steel for long life; the cap iron, which clamps over the iron to tension it and clear the shavings as they are produced; and the lever cap, which locates over a screw on the frog and clamps the whole assembly to the plane body.

A good-quality plane should be maintained whenever the blade is removed for sharpening. Clear all fragments of wood from the body, remove all dust and apply light machine oil to the moving parts.

### Jack plane
At 300–380mm (12–15in), this is a convenient size for most workshops. It is ideal for flattening the faces and edges of boards, and for preparing sawn timber (lumber).

Side adjustment

Frog

Mouth

Depth adjustment

Sole

Iron

Cap iron

Lever cap

### Smoothing plane
The most useful plane for fine finishing in all kinds of woodworking. It is usually 225–250mm (9–10in) long.

### Block plane

This is not classed as a true bench plane, although the body has a similar design. The blade has a much shallower angle and can be set for the removal of the finest shavings when working across end grain. A versatile tool, shaped to fit the palm of the hand and often used one-handed.

### Shoulder planes

(*above and right*) Each of these narrow planes has its blade set at an acute angle for the removal of fine shavings when trimming joints. They are essential tools when forming tenons or cleaning-up small rebates (rabbets).

### Compass plane

A very specialized plane with a flexible sole that can be formed into a shallow arc for working on curved surfaces.

### Rebate, or filister, plane (*right*)

The best plane for forming a rebate (rabbet) along the edge of a length of wood. Like the shoulder plane, its blade spans the full width of the body. Fitted with a sliding fence to control the width of the cut, and a depth stop.

### Plough plane (*below right*)

A more sophisticated version of the rebate (rabbet) plane, having interchangeable blades of different sizes. Can be used to form grooves or rebates (rabbets) with great accuracy. A combination plane will accept other blades, or cutters, of different profiles to form beaded and tongued mouldings.

### Spokeshave

This is a two-handed tool for working on rounded stock. Available with a flat base or a rounded base for dealing with convex or concave surfaces. The name comes from the days when wheelwrights made spokes for wooden wheels.

# POWER PLANERS AND ROUTERS

These are quite different tools to power saws, but they have in common the use
of rapidly rotating cutter blades, which remove the stock very quickly and easily.
When used safely they can be a powerful aid to most shaping operations.
Tungsten-carbide-tipped blades make it possible to work with manufactured
materials that can be very hardwearing on the sharpest of hand tools.

## Power planer key features:

- Reversible tungsten-carbide-tipped blades for longer life.
- Parallel fence for accurate rebating.
- Body design that allows a rebate (rabbet) depth up to 20mm (¾in).
- Dust extraction facility or collection bag for shavings.
- Automatic pivoting safety guard for cutter block.
- Safety switch and electronic speed control.
- V-groove in the sole plate to allow easy chamfering operations.

Power planer

**Power planer** This power tool is ideal
for the rapid removal of large amounts
of waste, but it should be handled
with great care, as it is extremely easy
to remove too much wood and ruin
the work. The depth of cut in one pass
ranges from 1.5 to 5mm (¹⁄₁₆ to ³⁄₁₆in) on
more powerful models; 3mm
(⅛in) is quite adequate for most
general purposes.

The cutter block, in which the
blades are mounted, rotates at very
high speed and should be treated with
great respect. Always make sure that
the power cord is well out of the way
when using a power planer, so that it
does not impede the work. Keep your
hands well away from the blades and
wait for the cutter block to stop
spinning before putting the tool down
on the workbench.

**Biscuit jointer** A biscuit jointer is a
handy tool for making quick work of
all kinds of jointing operation. The
"biscuits" are flat wooden dowels that
fit into semicircular slots formed by
the blade of the jointer. Its great
advantage is the ease with which
quick adjustments can be made to
suit any thickness of wood. The best
models have an adjustable carriage
that can be tilted up to 45 degrees for
dealing with mitred corners.

Biscuit jointer

**Router** A router is one of the most versatile and powerful tools a woodworker can have. It incorporates a rotary cutter mounted in an adjustable body, which removes small slices of wood with each rotation, allowing all kinds of profiling and shaping work.

The range of router cutters is huge, and a good way to begin is with a "starter" selection of ten or twelve cutters, which will cover a wide range of applications.

**Router key features:**

- Safety switch and "soft start" feature to prevent kick-back when starting.
- Variable speed control for different materials and delicate work.
- Stepped-adjustment depth gauge, allowing a series of passes at different depths.
- Dust extraction facility.
- Spindle lock for easy cutter changing.
- Range of collets to receive cutters of different shank sizes: 6–12mm (¼–½in).
- Parallel fence with fine tuning adjustment.
- Template follower for copying patterns and routing curves.

**Router table** More powerful routers can be mounted upside-down in a work table, allowing very efficient machining operations. With a sliding fence and protective cutter guard, continuous profiling work will be accurate and safe. Large-diameter professional cutters make short work of mouldings and tongued-and-grooved panels.

Router

Router table

# CHISELS

A high-quality forged steel blade set in a tough handle are the qualities to look for in a good woodworking chisel. Traditional chisels with hardwood handles should only be struck with a wooden mallet; more modern versions with shatter-resistant polypropylene handles can withstand hammer blows equally well. Most chisels are available in matched sets, ranging in size from 6 to 38mm (¼ to 1½in) or more, but for a more modest outlay, a set of three, comprising the most useful sizes of 12, 19 and 25mm (½, ¾ and 1in), will suffice.

### Bevelled chisels

Bevel-edge, or bevelled, chisels are the most versatile type you can buy for most woodworking tasks. They can be used for chopping out material when struck with a mallet, or for more gentle paring and shaping tasks when used freehand. A newly purchased chisel will have the main bevel ground on the end of its blade, but a secondary bevel will need adding to hone it ready for use.

| 32mm | 25mm | 19mm | 12mm | 10mm | 6mm |
| (1¼in) | (1in) | (¾in) | (½in) | (⅜in) | (¼in) |

### Firmer chisels

A firmer chisel is just that: a stronger blade designed to accept heavier blows when chopping out a mortise or socket. The end bevel is designed for slicing across the end grain of wood, while the long edges are not bevelled, allowing the cutting of square, parallel-sided mortises. Usually, firmer chisels are sold only in four common sizes to suit the standard widths of mortise used in general joinery. Good quality steel is essential for these chisels, to give a good sharp edge, which can withstand heavy use.

| 25mm | 19mm | 12mm | 6mm |
| (1in) | (¾in) | (½in) | (¼in) |

## Gouges

Although gouges are used principally for carving, most woodworkers will have one or two in their toolkits for dealing with curved mouldings and other shaping operations.

Gouges can be bevelled on the outer, convex surface of the cutting edge (out-cannel gouge), for most grooving actions, or on the concave surface (in-cannel gouge) for paring, trimming and carving.

| 25mm | 19mm | 12mm | 6mm | 25mm | 19mm | 12mm | 6mm |
|------|------|------|-----|------|------|------|-----|
| (1in) | (¾in) | (½in) | (¼in) | (1in) | (¾in) | (½in) | (¼in) |

## Sharpening equipment

A good sharpening stone is a vital part of the toolkit. Without a sharp edge, a chisel will be not only difficult to work with, but also dangerous. The chisel will follow where the wood directs it, rather than where you want it to go, and can easily slip.

Chisels should be sharpened at the beginning and end of every session. If they are attended to regularly, just a few minutes' work will keep the honed edges in prime condition. Once in a while, a longer honing session might be necessary – if the bevel loses its original angle or if the edge is chipped.

Natural sharpening stones are quite expensive, and synthetic versions are commonly used. Japanese water stones are of natural stone and need water as a lubricant. They can produce a finely ground edge on the best-quality steel. For more general use, oilstones are sufficient.

A combination stone is the best buy, two stones of different grades being bonded together back to back.

The coarse stone is for regrinding to the correct bevel; the fine stone for delivering a keen honed edge. A honing guide is a useful accessory and will assist in maintaining the correct angle of a chisel or plane iron when being sharpened. By clamping the blade in the guide and moving it gently to and fro on the stone, you will be able to grind a constant angle without difficulty.

Conical and cylindrical slipstones and wedges are sometimes used to achieve the correct profile on the blades of curved and angled chisels.

Combination stone

Combination stone

Japanese water stone

Honing guide

Wedge

45

# HAND DRILLS

There are few woodworking projects that do not require drilling holes of some kind, if only for fixing screws. To insert a screw correctly, a clearance hole should be drilled in the piece to be fixed to match the size of the screw's shank and prevent the wood from splitting as the screw is tightened. A countersink or counterbore may also be needed to sink the head of the screw below the surface. Finally, a pilot hole is usually advisable, of the correct diameter to suit the tapered, threaded end of the screw. All these operations can be carried out easily with a hand drill.

## Accurate drilling

This is an important woodworking technique, and it has been much simplified in recent years with powered hand drills and even more so with bench-mounted pillar drills. Hand drilling with a brace still has a place, however, especially in sites far removed from electric power. Even in the workshop, it is often quicker to reach for a small hand drill than to set up a power drill just for the few holes required before proceeding to the next stage of the job.

**Hand drill** A useful tool for quickly producing small holes when needed. Ideal for drilling pilot holes and countersinking. Its small size comes in handy in tight corners.

### Practical tip

Never interfere with the centre point of a drill if it has one – this will almost certainly affect its concentricity.

**Gimlet** The screw thread is for starting a screw hole without fear of splitting the wood when the screw is inserted.

**Carpenter's brace** This is a powerful drilling tool, which provides ample leverage from the wide sweep of its handle. Look for a "universal" jaw – a chuck that accepts both tapered and parallel drill bits – and a reversible ratchet action.

**Bradawl** Sharp pointed shaft for scribing and piercing holes for pins and nails.

## Drill bits

Great advances have also been made in the pattern of bits and there are now bits especially designed for setting dowels. This technique is often used in projects involving manufactured boards such as chipboard or ply and these produce flat-bottomed holes. There are also flat bits, which work with a scraping action and cut large holes very rapidly, although these are not as accurate as twist bits. For the home worker on a limited budget, an adjustable bit is a good investment but these can only be used in a hand brace and not in any powered tool. The ordinary twist bit is used for making small holes and for starting screws. Beware of buying cheap sets of drill bits. They can be made of poor-quality steel and can be easily blunted.

**Standard twist drills** (*left*) Sometimes described as HSS (high-speed steel), these bore holes easily in steel, but are equally suitable for woodworking. They are made in a wide range of sizes at small increments – 1mm (¹⁄₃₂in) – so there should be no difficulty in finding the correct size.

**Spade, or flat, bits** (*right*) These are the traditional woodworker's drill bit for larger holes up to 32mm (1¼in) in diameter. Drill vertically, using a brace, for best results.

**Centre-point (brad point), or "lip and spur", bits** (*right*) These should only be used for wood. The point centres the bit exactly, preventing slipping and helping to keep the hole straight as you work. Made in a smaller range of sizes than standard twist drills, but still adequate for most needs. They are also known as dowel drill bits, as certain diameters match the small wooden dowels used for aligning joints – 6, 8 and 10mm (¼, ⁵⁄₁₆ and ⅜in).

# POWER DRILLS

**For any repetitive work, or removing large amounts of waste, a power drill is essential. Certain types of drill bit are designed specifically for use at high speeds and will not produce satisfactory results in a hand drill. Sometimes, a low speed with high torque, or turning force, is the best combination, and a power drill of the correct rating is ideal for this. The power source of the drill is all important – motors range in capacity from 300 watts (3 amp) for light duty to 1000 watts (10 amp) and above for really heavy work; a 600 watt (6 amp) motor is fine for general duties. A motor will soon burn out if the drill is overloaded.**

Cordless drill

**Cordless drill** One of the first items in your toolkit should be a cordless drill. These are relatively recent products, but in the space of ten years or so they have been found to be so useful that there is now a vast range on the market. One of the advantages for the woodworker is that many cordless drills can be used as slow speed, powered screwdrivers.

The voltage of the battery determines the power of the drill and the length of time it can be used before recharging. Top-of-the-range models have 18 volt batteries – 9.6 or 12 volt is adequate for general use. Always check the manufacturer's instruction manual.

### Cordless drill key features:

- Spare battery, allowing uninterrupted use without having to wait for recharging.
- Carrying case and rapid charger.
- 10mm (⅜in) keyless chuck, allowing quick changing of drill bits.
- Screwdriver bits, clipped to the body of the drill when not in use.
- Two-speed or variable-speed facility.
- Reversible action (essential for screwdriving).
- Adjustable torque control to prevent breaking screws.
- Electric brake that stops rotation instantly when the trigger is released.

**Electric drill** For more regular use, there is no substitute for a power drill operating on mains voltage. This will run continuously at higher speeds and is ideal for mounting in a drill stand. Many power drills have a percussion facility useful for drilling into masonry, stone or brick, but this can be switched off for normal use when working with wood. A depth gauge is useful, as is a variable-speed/reversible action. A side handle provides extra grip and makes it easier to hold the drill vertical when used freehand. Some drills even have a side handle containing a small spirit level for greater accuracy. The extra power means that a 13mm (½in) chuck can be fitted to accommodate the largest drill bits.

Electric drill

**Percussion drill** A hammer, or percussion, drill is only required for drilling into masonry, using specially hardened masonry bits. It will be useful for installing items that need fixing to plaster or brickwork, but unless you intend doing a lot of work of this kind it could be an expensive luxury. Consider renting one when necessary – do not be tempted to overload a smaller drill that is not designed for heavy duty use.

Percussion drill

### Specialized drill bits

Plug cutters are a useful addition to any workshop, especially where quality work is undertaken. Another common accessory to drilling is the countersink. This allows the head of a screw to be sunk cleanly flush with the surface of the wood.

Forstner bits are designed to drill large flat-bottomed holes that do not go through the wood, such as might be needed to fit kitchen cabinet hinges. They are also accurate for drilling deep holes even in the end grain of timber.

**Boring bit** Used for boring holes for concealed hinges or other fittings of a standard size. Available in 25 and 35mm (1 and 1⅜in) diameters. Drills a shallow, flat-bottomed hole, with a centre point to keep it centred accurately.

**Counterbore, or 3-in-1, bit** This device will drill a pilot hole, clearance hole and counterbore for a screw in one operation. Obtainable in different sizes to suit a range of screws and usually sold with a plug cutter of the same gauge.

**Plug cutter** This makes small wooden plugs for concealing fixings. Ideally, it should be used in a drill stand, as it is not self-centring.

**Countersink bit** A "rosehead" countersink creates a recess for the screw head so that it is flush with the surface. Use with care, as it is very easy to spoil the work by drilling too deep.

**Masonry bits** Available in many different sizes. You will need to use this bit when attaching fittings for wooden cupboards, shelves and other types of furniture to masonry walls.

**Circular hole cutter** This must be used in a fixed drill stand or a drill with an additional side-mounted handle for safety. Select a low drill speed with a high torque setting, as the teeth remove a large amount of waste. Various sizes are available and fit a common arbor, which contains a 6mm (¼in) pilot drill to centre the hole. Holes up to 100mm (4in) in diameter are possible.

**Auger bit** This will drill deep holes quickly, removing waste. If used with a power drill, the motor must have a reverse facility, otherwise you will not be able to remove it.

# TOOLS FOR FIXING

**No tool box is complete without a hammer and a screwdriver for straightforward assembly work. There are different types to suit every need. Even though they are familiar items, they should be selected and used carefully.**

### Hammers

The head, or poll, of a hammer should be of good quality steel, heat treated and hardened for a long life. Hammer sizes are ranged by weight measured in ounces, even in these days of metrication: from 4oz for a small pin hammer up to 20oz.

**Cross pein, or pin, hammer** The small cross pein opposite the striking face comes into its own when fixing small panel pins (brads). Hold each pin between finger and thumb, and the narrow blade will be small enough to slide between them to deliver a few gentle taps to start it.

**Ball pein hammer**
More of an engineer's tool; the most heavy-duty hammer in common use and not often called for in woodworking.

**Rubber mallet** A useful tool for assembly work, when a reasonably firm blow may be required to knock a component into position. The rubber head will not bruise the surface of the wood. You can also buy a dead-blow mallet, which is a synthetic hammer with a hollow head, which is filled with lead shot. It delivers a sharp blow with little effort and no bounce. It is useful for assembly work.

**Carpenter's mallet** A solid beech mallet is of the correct strength and density to deliver a sound blow to a chisel without jarring. An essential tool for any carpenter.

**Claw hammer** A good-quality traditional claw hammer has a handle made of hickory, selected for its great shock-resistant properties. The precision-ground head should be fixed firmly to the shaft with hardwood and iron wedges, and feel well balanced for driving nails straight.

Slotted screwdrivers (*left*) and cross-head (Phillips) screwdrivers (*right*)

## Screwdrivers

Screws come in all shapes and sizes, with different types of head, and there are just as many types of screwdriver to suit them. The quickest way to strip the head of a screw is to use a screwdriver that does not match. Worse still, it can slip out of position and damage the work. Screwdrivers with interchangeable bits, which can be quickly inserted into a socket on the screwdriver shaft, make life easier, but there is still no substitute for the traditional cabinet-maker's tool.

Screw heads vary in size according to their gauge, common sizes ranging from a No.4 (the smallest) up to a No.12 or greater, and you will find a screwdriver to fit each perfectly. A longer shaft will provide more torque; a short screwdriver makes up for this with a larger handle for extra grip. Slotted screws are steadily being replaced by screws with cross-heads, which prevent the driver from slipping out of position, provided it is of the correct size. Make sure you have a set of screwdrivers handy to cover most needs. Never use a screwdriver blade as a lever to open a can of paint – the tip of the blade is tempered steel and can easily shatter if misused.

## Screwdriver bits

Small bits with hexagonal shafts are designed for use in special socketed handles, but some can also be clamped into the chuck of a cordless power drill.

A selection of driver bits will take up far less space than a set of separate screwdrivers. They range from long bits for heavy-duty work to short, 25mm (1in) bits, which must be fitted in a holder. All have a standard 6mm (¼in) hexagonal shank. A magnetic bit holder makes quick work of changing bits and will hold a steel screw on the tip for one-handed operation. Cross-head screws are available in two

*Above* Screwdrivers range considerably in size, from large heavy-duty drivers with a flared tip to the smallest stubby screwdrivers. The tips are described according to the size of screw they are designed for: gauge sizes for slotted screws, and point sizes for cross-heads.

types, which require different screwdrivers. A Phillips head has a simple four-way cross design, while the Pozidriv version gives a more positive grip with four additional flutes between the main slots.

It is important to be able to recognize the difference and select the right bit to suit the screw, otherwise the head will strip as you tighten up the screw.

Double-ended bits

Long heavy-duty bits    Phillips-head bits    Pozidriv-head bits    Flat bits

# ABRASIVE PAPERS AND SCRAPERS

**"Sandpaper" has always been used to give a final finish for wood, although it is not made with sand. Small abrasive particles, glued to a backing paper, are graded according to their size: the finer the grit, the smoother the finish. Grades range from 40 grit up to 1200 grit, so fine that sometimes it is called flour paper in some countries.**

### Varieties of paper

Many different types of material are used to make abrasive papers. For the woodworker, the most useful include garnet paper, silicon carbide and aluminium oxide paper. Garnet paper is dark red in colour and fairly coarse. It is used for flattening rough-sawn surfaces. Glass paper is paler in colour and available in the full range of grit sizes. It tends to wear quite quickly, but is economical to use.

Silicon carbide paper is more hardwearing and quite efficient. Light grey silicon paper is self-lubricating, providing a smoother finish. Dark grey paper is sometimes called "wet and dry" paper and needs lubricating with water. It is available right up to 1200 grit and is used for fine finishing.

Aluminium oxide paper is sometimes called production paper. It is the hardest wearing material and is the best option for heavy-duty use. However, it is not generally available in much finer grades than 180 grit. For woodworkers, the grades of silicon carbide and aluminium oxide papers most used are 80, 100, 120, 150, 180, 240 and 320 grit.

Use a square of sandpaper wrapped around a cork or rubber sanding block for best results. A small wooden block can be used with some success, but using a more flexible material allows better control and reduces wear on the paper, making it last longer. Make sure the face of the block is free of defects to avoid scoring the surface of the work.

Aluminium oxide papers     Silicon carbide papers     Glass papers     Garnet papers

## Scrapers

A cabinet scraper works by cutting the wood fibres rather than wearing them down through abrasion, but is capable of delivering a very smooth finish. It is well worth acquiring the knack of sharpening and using one. A set of scrapers of different profiles will allow the finishing of curved and moulded surfaces. Whereas sandpaper tends to round off sharp edges, the profile of a gooseneck scraper can be matched to almost any curved moulding, thus preserving fine details.

Flat cabinet scraper

Convex/concave scraper

Gooseneck scraper

## Rasps

Rasps are useful for roughing out or smoothing the edges of wood when working freehand. A wood file can then be used to achieve a finer finish. Both tools come into their own if you are dealing with variable or uneven grain where using a plane produces poor results. They can be flat or round, and a half-round profile is the most versatile. The pointed end of the file is the tang, and is generally fitted into a separate wooden handle. A surform rasp has holes in its teeth and does not clog up as much as normal rasps.

## Wire (steel) wool

This is useful for final finishing. It is available in nine grades and from 5 at the coarse end for stripping and 0000 at the fine end. It is clog resistant.

Rasp

File

Rasp handle

Wire (steel) wool

# POWER SANDERS

**These come in two main types. Belt sanders employ a cloth-backed sanding belt, usually of fairly coarse grade, for the rapid removal of stock. Orbital sanders have a backing pad that makes rapid circular movements and is capable of fine finishing work.**

**Belt sander** This should be used with great care, as it can easily dig in to the surface, leaving deep scour marks. The most important feature to look for is efficient dust extraction, as large amounts of waste are produced. A dust collection bag is essential, but the facility for connecting to an extractor unit is even better.

Different models of belt sander use belts of varying sizes, and for some reason no common standard size has been adopted by manufacturers, so check that the belt size you need is widely available.

### Belt sander key features:

- Two-speed or variable-speed motor to suit different surfaces.
- Automatic tracking control to keep the belt running smoothly.

Belt sander

**Orbital sander** More useful than a belt sander for general use. The sanding action is less severe, and by using progressively finer grades of paper, a fine finish can be achieved. Three common sizes of sander are available: half-sheet, one-third sheet and quarter-sheet. These denote the size of sandpaper that needs cutting from a standard sheet thus avoiding waste.

### Orbital sander key features:

- Effective dust collection pouch.
- Perforated base and sanding sheets that prevent dust from collecting under the sander.
- Quick-release clips for changing sanding sheets.
- Variable speed for delicate work.

Orbital sander

## Multi-function sanders

For intricate modelling and restoration work, a family of sanders with specially shaped sanding pads are worth considering. Delta sanders have a triangular base ideal for reaching into the corners of panels. Self-adhesive sanding sheets can be changed quickly without clips, but are more expensive.

Multi-function sanders

**Palm sander** This allows one-handed operation and is not suitable for heavy work, but it is ideal for a light touch to produce a fine finish. The sanding base vibrates at a higher speed than a large orbital sander. It takes quarter-sheet of standard sized sandpaper, and as with larger models, a dust-collection pouch is advisable.

Palm sander

**Random orbit sander** This is a versatile tool, combining two functions in one. Hold the sander lightly and the circular sanding disc spins in a circular motion for the rapid removal of rough surfaces. Apply more pressure and the action changes to a reciprocating orbital motion for finer finishing.

Random orbit sander

# CLAMPS, TOOLBOXES AND WORKBENCHES

There are many varieties to meet the needs of different workshop tasks. Most woodworking adhesives depend on high pressure to form a solid bond and need to be clamped for long periods. Clamps have other uses, too, such as locating components temporarily when setting out and holding wood steady while working. Clamping the work firmly before any operation is a vital part of safe woodworking practice. The well-equipped workshop will have a collection of several types and sizes of clamp.

**Sash (bar) clamp** (*above*) Two clamp heads on a steel bar deliver firm parallel pressure, on which accurate joinery depends. Available in lengths up to 1.2m (4ft) and more, and most useful when employed in pairs.

**G-clamp** (*above*) The traditional woodworker's tool – you can never have too many G-clamps. Good-quality forged steel is essential; cheaper cast versions can shatter if overtightened.

**Mitre (frame) clamp** (*above*) A specialized tool that is ideal for frame making. Slide two components together to meet at the centre of the clamp, which guarantees a true right angle.

**Web clamp** (*below*) Useful for furniture making and assembling objects of irregular shape. The strong nylon webbing extends around the work and is tightened with a small spanner (wrench), applying tension equally around the assembly.

**F-clamps, or screw clamps** (*above*)
These versatile clamps are quickly adjustable. Slide the movable arm along the bar until it locks against the work, then tighten the screw.

**Quick (spring) clamp** (*above*) This only applies light pressure, but is useful for a temporary fixing, as it can be used one-handed, leaving the other hand free to locate the components.

## Toolboxes

Good tools need to be well organized and protected from damage. In earlier times, the first task of the woodwork apprentice was to make his own toolchest or toolbox, designed for his own personal toolkit. A simple box made from a few pieces of plywood, with internal compartments to keep tools separated, is well worth making when time allows. Alternatively, there is a good range of ready-made items to choose from.

A robust steel engineer's toolbox is good for smaller hand tools, with easily accessible compartments in a compact form.

Cheaper versions in rigid plastic are useful for keeping screws and nails tidy and ready for use.

Larger tools, such as hand saws and planes, can be protected in a heavy-duty canvas toolbag, while a leather tool roll is ideal for chisels. When buying a power tool, a purpose-made carrying case is a good option to look for. It will keep the tool free of dust and protect the power cord.

Engineer's toolbox

Plastic toolbox with separate compartments

## Workbenches

A good workbench will have a solid flat top with a vice fixed at one end. Even in the workshop a folding portable workbench comes into its own as a temporary support. The adjustable jaws are ideal for clamping lengths of timber (lumber).

A foldaway portable workbench

A permanent wooden workbench

# MACHINE TOOLS

Equipping a professional workshop with heavy-duty machine tools is a costly process, but the serious woodworker can benefit from smaller versions, designed for semi-professional and home workshop use. For your own safety, these machines should not be used without proper training. Many local technical schools and colleges offer evening courses in woodworking, and this is a good way to learn the principles of operating powerful machinery and to expand your abilities. If your workshop space and budget allows, this overview of woodworking machinery will give you an idea of the most popular machines and their function.

**Saw bench (Table saw)** The heart of a workshop, allowing solid timber (lumber) and sheet materials to be cut to precise dimensions with ease. The saw motor is mounted beneath the table, having a rise-and-fall action to control the height of the blade and a tilting carriage for cutting angles up to 45 degrees. A parallel fence, which slides on a calibrated scale, allows quick adjustment.

**Bandsaw** (*right*) A continuous blade of flexible steel, running through an adjustable table, makes all kinds of woodworking operations possible. A bandsaw is less powerful than a circular saw, but capable of ripping wide boards lengthways to produce thinner stock, crosscutting, and cutting curves and angles.

**Jointer surfacer** A separate machine that produces straight, square stock, as with a planer thicknesser, but removes the necessity to reset the machinery for dual operation. It is ideal for producing square-edged boards for joining together in wide panels.

**Radial saw** (*right*) A circular saw body mounted overhead on a radial arm; ideal for continuous crosscutting work. The arm can also be swivelled through 90 degrees, permitting ripsawing and angled cuts.

**Morticer** (*above*) A real time-saver when making mortises. An auger revolves in a square chisel, removing waste and forming a perfectly square mortise. The key to accurate work is a solid table that keeps the work square to the direction of cut at all times.

**Planer thicknesser (Combination jointer)** (*right*) One of the most useful machines for the home workshop. Two sets of operations are possible. On the overhead table (jointer), a length of timber (lumber) is fed over the cutter block, which is exactly square to the side fence. This produces a perfectly square edge on rough stock as a first stage. Below the table, a length of timber is fed between an adjustable bed and the rotating cutter block to produce parallel, smooth faces to accurate dimensions.

**Lathe** (*left*) Unlike any other machine tool, the lathe makes possible a whole new dimension of woodworking, by turning the stock lengthways against the tool. Any cylindrical form can be produced, from spindles to bowls and goblets.

**Spindle moulder** (*left*) Similar to a powerful router. The spindle carries a set of steel cutters, revolving at high speed, for making mouldings and shaping wood. A high degree of precision is possible, allowing the production of large quantities of profiles with consistent accuracy.

**Pillar drill (Drill press)** (*above*) A heavy-duty drilling machine with an adjustable table; perfect for repetitive drilling work with consistent accuracy. Multi-speed for working with different materials, and controllable for drilling blind holes to an accurate fixed depth.

# GETTING STARTED

No one simply decides one day to become a woodworker. The introduction to the craft of woodworking is a gradual process, as one increasingly finds that handling and working with wood produces a feeling of satisfaction and reward.

A useful way to begin is to use ready-made plans to make something you need or that you find attractive, where the design and method of construction are already worked out. It will become more important to understand how and why things are done in a certain way, and to broaden your experience with other projects, different types of wood or new tools and techniques. From there, it is a small step to want to make variations, try out new ideas and develop your own designs.

There is no need to feel restricted by a fixed set of rules – the attraction of working with wood stems from the infinite possibilities that the material offers. Nevertheless, certain principles should be followed to avoid early disappointment. This chapter provides an introduction to the planning and design process, and gives a few pointers to safe and successful woodworking practice.

# WORKSHOP PLANNING

The novice woodworker might start out by working on a portable workbench in the backyard, a garage or a spare room, only to discover the frustrations of limited space and lack of opportunity to tackle more elaborate projects. Defining a viable workspace, whatever its size, is the first step to working safely and efficiently. A workshop will often be expanded as one's skills and ambitions develop, but if this happens without forethought, confusion and inefficiency are inevitable.

**Benchhook**

### Workbenches

The centre of operations for any woodworker is the workbench. Above all, it must be stable and able to resist the forces applied to the work when clamped to it. Also, it must have a perfectly flat top for accurate assembly tasks. If the surface of the workbench is not true, it cannot be relied on for setting out accurate joinery: anything you make on it will reflect the deformity when assembled.

Hardwood workbenches can be purchased in a kit form at fairly low cost, or you can make one yourself along the same lines. A good workbench will have a solid flat top

with a vice fixed at one end. For a right-handed woodworker, the left side of the bench is the best position for the vice. Holes at suitable intervals in the top of the bench act as locations for "dogs", or bench stops, against which a piece of wood can be wedged to hold it while planing or sawing. The traditional bench has a recessed well along the back edge to store tools while working.

A drawer for small items that otherwise may go astray is well worth having, while a stout lower shelf will help to stiffen the construction and keep it square. Strong legs provide support – when hammering or using a

mallet, the work should be positioned directly over one corner to avoid straining the top. Some woodworkers prefer to attach a "sacrificial" top of cheap plywood, which can be replaced from time to time as it wears.

### Bench accessories

A vital piece of equipment is a bench vice, which should be of good quality as it is a precision instrument for holding your work squarely and securely. A woodworking vice can be obtained as a separate item from any tool shop and fitted to your own bench if required.

You can add a variety of useful accessories to a workbench, such as a simple tool rack made from a strip of plywood and a series of hardwood blocks screwed to the end of the bench. A bench hook is a square of plywood with a lip that hooks over the front of the bench, and a backstop to support the work.

Screw a board to the wall directly above the workbench for storing other tools and workshop items. Fit it with spring clips for holding chisels and screwdrivers, and wooden pegs for suspending hand saws.

**Workbench**

Bench dog

Well

Tool rack

Bench hook

Vice

### Practical tip

Spend time getting your bench at exactly the height that suits you. An incorrect height can prove to be tiring. Never shorten the legs of a bench if it is too high, work off a duckboard if necessary.

## Workshop layout

If you have plenty of space at your disposal, give some thought to the overall layout of the workshop. Think of the route taken by the wood as it is worked into the finished article, and treat the workshop as a small production line, with separate areas for each stage of the operation.

Setting out your work needs a large flat area along one side. The workbench, with tool or wood storage above, should be alongside this, with a clear space in the centre for any tasks involving power or machine tools. Keep the finishing area separate from the work area and, if possible, behind a partition to keep dust to a minimum. Use a dust extractor when creating large quantities of shavings or fine sawdust.

If you have room for a sawbench (table saw) or other machinery, a central position with plenty of clear space around it will be required to accommodate large sheets of plywood and long lengths of timber. Build a table at the right height to support the work as it passes beyond the saw, and economize on space by using the same area for feeding planed timber back toward the saw in a circular route. The table can also act as an assembly area for large projects, with good access from all sides and room for timber storage below.

Drill stand

Mortiser

Workbenches

Planer thicknesser

Band saw

Shelving and
tool storage

Timber
storage

Assembly area

Dust extraction

Wall cupboards

Finishing area

Saw table

Desk and
drawing board

Fire extinguisher

# HEALTH AND SAFETY

Your personal safety should underlie every stage of woodworking practice, including the layout of a workshop. It is better to plan your work to eliminate hazards rather than accommodate them – for example, using a dust extractor on a machine that creates a lot of dust is a better solution than wearing a dust mask. Because woodworking depends on the use of cutting tools, this may seem a risk that cannot be avoided, but any experienced craftsman will confirm that a sharp tool is actually less dangerous than a blunt one or a tool that is used incorrectly.

Fire extinguisher

## Working practice

Working safely is largely a matter of common sense and awareness. More accidents occur as a result of losing concentration than for any other reason. Develop a sense of rhythm and routine when working, so that you are in tune with what you are doing. Never rush to finish a job, whatever the motivation. There is no advantage in quick results if you risk ruining the work, not to mention suffering injury.

If someone enters your workshop while you are working, finish the task and switch off any machinery before addressing them. They will soon learn to follow your work discipline. For obvious reasons, do not lock yourself in to avoid being disturbed when working alone. On the other hand, do keep the workshop locked in your absence for the safety of others.

### Personal safety

Avoid wearing loose clothing and jewellery when working, especially with machinery and power tools. A stout pair of boots should be worn in case of accidents – a sheet of plywood will be painful if it slips and lands on your toe. You can prevent this by wearing a pair of leather or canvas gloves when handling timber. Always inspect a piece of wood for splinters and protruding nails before picking it up. Always have a first aid kit in the workshop for minor injuries. When you work on large machines, do not work alone in case of injury.

## Workshop safety

Observe the following points to reduce the risk of accidents:

**Keep the workshop tidy** An obvious point, but at times it may be tempting to leave the chore of sweeping up until another day. Make a habit of tidying the workshop at the end of every session and dispose of dust and debris sensibly. Keep a check on small offcuts (scraps) that tend to collect wherever you are working and present a real hazard underfoot. Wood and sawdust are biodegradable, so they can be disposed of easily at a local recycling depot.

**Treat chemical waste with care** Many finishing products are inflammable or harmful to the environment and should be stored separately in a secure place, inaccessible to children and animals. Used chemicals should be collected in resealable containers and disposed of safely at an appropriate waste depot. This even applies to finishing cloths and wipes. Certain volatile products are highly inflammable in concentrated form; spread out contaminated rags so that solvents can evaporate before disposal.

**Consider the fire risk** Avoiding all naked flames can reduce the risk of fire and, it goes without saying, the workshop should be a non-smoking zone. Install a powder-filled fire extinguisher at every exit door, and fit a smoke alarm. A pile of sawdust can smoulder for hours before bursting into flame. A well-kept workshop has no piles of sawdust, of course, but a smoke alarm guarantees peace of mind.

**Observe electrical safety** Install a safe power circuit, protected by a circuit breaker to cut off the power in case of any wiring fault or accident. Make sure the circuit is adequate for the load of any machines likely to be used, and fit a master switch near the entrance to the workshop so that switching off all the power becomes routine at the end of every session.

Extension cords trailing across the floor are common causes of accidents, so keep them clipped out of harm's way if they have to be used. Examine all power cords regularly for wear, replacing any that have damaged outer sleeving. Make sure the workshop is well lit with bright fluorescent lighting.

## Safety equipment

Even though a private workshop is not required to comply with health and safety legislation, which applies to commercial premises, it makes sense to observe the same safety disciplines and use the personal protection equipment that is recommended and readily available.

**First aid kit** Obtain the correct size of kit recommended for small workshops, and keep it in a prominent position ready for use. If any of the contents are used, replace them immediately.

**Eye protection** Always protect your eyes with safety glasses or goggles when sanding, finishing or using power tools. When operating a machine that produces large quantities of chippings at high speed, wear a full-face visor.

**Ear protection** When using power tools or machinery, wear approved ear defenders (protectors) or earplugs to keep noise to an acceptable level. Some people think that it is safer to operate a machine by listening to its performance. They are wrong, and they risk permanent impairment of their hearing in the future.

**Dust masks** There are several types of mask to choose from, including the frame mask with replaceable pads and disposable masks that cover the whole of the mouth and nose. Choose the right product for the level of dust generated in the workshop. The dust produced by sanding machines is the most hazardous and needs a mask with a fine filter. Use sanders that are fitted with their own dust collection bag to cut down on the amount of dust produced. Clear, full-face safety masks are available now and are easy to put on and comfortable to wear, especially when using power tools.

When working with hazardous finishing materials, keep the workshop well ventilated and wear a respirator if necessary. Always be guided by the manufacturer's safety data, which by

law must be supplied with any hazardous product. In general, if a product is so dangerous as to cause serious problems, you should consider an alternative.

**Gloves and boots** It is advisable to wear heavy-duty rigger's gloves when handling sawn timber (lumber) or large, heavy sheets of material. When you are using adhesives or finishing materials that are harmful to the skin, wear rubber or latex gloves. It is best to wear sensible and sturdy boots to keep toes protected in case you drop any wood.

*Above* Wear gloves when handling large pieces of wood.

## Dust extraction

By far the best way of reducing the risk of inhaling sawdust is to install a dust extraction system. Compact units designed for the small workshop are available from all good tool suppliers. Many portable power tools are supplied with adaptors for direct connection to an extraction unit.

# PLANS AND DRAWINGS

**Drawing plans before starting a job is an important part of the design process. They will help you to visualize how the different components of your woodworking project fit together and how the two dimensions on the paper are translated into the three dimensions of a solid object. They also take the guesswork out of calculating the quantity of materials required, keeping costs down. No special skills are required, merely the same methodical approach that is part of any woodworking operation. Even a quick sketch on the back of an envelope can be enough to clarify an idea or reveal any discrepancies of scale or measurement before proceeding.**

### Views

These are usually the most helpful drawings when designing a project. The plan view shows the object viewed from above, and the elevation as viewed from one side. A section view shows a slice through the object. For a complex design with many components you may need more than one section to develop the idea.

There is no need to spend a long time on a complicated piece of artwork – a good drawing shows just the right amount of detail, clearly set out, and no more. Include the scale you have used to avoid errors and get a feel for the proportions of the design.

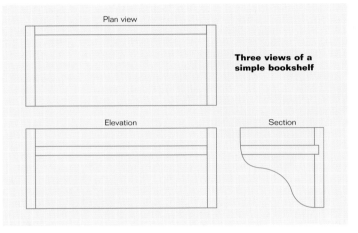

Plan view

**Three views of a simple bookshelf**

Elevation

Section

*Left* All of these items will prove invaluable for drawing plans for your projects: graph paper – useful for scale drawings and templates; plain paper or a sketch pad; a clipboard or drawing board; masking tape; a pair of compasses (compass); dividers or callipers – for the accurate transfer and duplication of measurements; drawing pens, pencils and a carpenter's pencil; eraser and pencil sharpener; a set square and protractor; templates for circular cutouts or other necessary shapes; rules (imperial or metric scales); scale rule and a pocket calculator for converting measurements and making calculations.

## Scale drawings

Scale drawings are the best way to design a job accurately. They will allow you to get a feel for the proportions of the finished article. A scale rule converts dimensions on to the paper automatically; otherwise an ordinary rule can be used for simple scales such as 1:10 (when working in metric units) or 1:12 (imperial units – 1in equals 12in). You can also use graph paper, in either metric or imperial scales, to establish a grid on to which quite complex shapes may be plotted. Choose any scale that allows the overall dimensions of the object to fit neatly on the page.

## Cutting lists and plans

From an accurate scale drawing, it is easy to work out a detailed cutting (cut) list for all the materials needed for a project. This helps when selecting the wood, making sure that you do not run short. When making an item where the grain of the timber is to be displayed at its best, it is important to purchase one batch of material so that all the components are of a matching colour and figure.

Label each part to identify it on the cutting list, and mark each piece of wood as it is finished to avoid confusion. Record any alterations you make on the cutting list and file it away safely as you might want to repeat the project in the future or use it as the basis for a similar job.

Cutting plans are slightly different: if you need to cut large sheets of plywood or MDF (medium-density fibreboard) into a set of different sized pieces, it is worth taking a few minutes to sketch out the most efficient layout to avoid waste.

All components of a similar width, for example, can be cut from one strip, then cross cut to length one at a time. Try combining different sizes to make up the full width or length of a sheet so offcuts (scraps) are kept to bare minimum.

## Scaling-up

When dealing with complex curved profiles, it is useful to be able to scale-up a detail to produce a working template. Make a tracing of the small-scale drawing and lay it over a sheet of graph paper. Then transfer each section to a similar grid on a larger scale to reproduce the full-size pattern. The more intricate the design, the finer the grid should be to capture every detail.

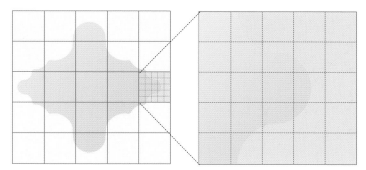

## Isometrics

This simply means "of equal measurement". An isometric drawing does not give a true idea of shape or perspective, but to the draughtsman or designer it is invaluable, allowing true measurements to be scaled from a drawing in all three dimensions. Simply divide a circle into three equal segments of 120 degrees to establish an axis for each side of a three dimensional object. When drawn to this format, the exact measurements in any direction can be reproduced faithfully on the page to establish how a construction will fit together.

**Isometric axes**

**Isometric sketch**

# DESIGN

**Wood has so many variable qualities and such wide potential as a construction material that it is difficult to make any hard and fast design rules. Every piece of work is unique, and a common creed among woodworkers is to allow the wood to "speak for itself" and the natural qualities of each piece to suggest the best way of using it.**

### Grain direction

The pleasure of woodworking lies in working with it and not against it to express organic forms. Designing around the material in this way is an intriguing process of developing ideas in new and unexpected directions. As you will generally not be making free-form sculpture, to produce a well-constructed design requires the careful selection of material, tools and techniques to achieve the best results. Over the years, certain species of wood have become associated with specific types of furniture for the qualities they possess.

When working a piece of wood with hand tools, you will discover that it will behave better when cut or shaped in a particular direction, and can be most "unfriendly" if you try to force it in another. Thus, you should have no qualms about altering a design to reflect this changing quality as you work; this is one reason why no two pieces of work will be the same.

*Right* Directional table by Christopher Rose, made from maple with a veneered top and detachable solid leg frames.
*Below* Boxwood stringing provides a hardwearing edge to this steamed pear desk by Nicholas Pryke.

### Design properties of wood

*Beech* was used for making chairs because of its good bending properties. The resistance to splitting of *elm*, with its knotty grain, makes it ideal for chair seats and table tops. *Ash* possesses a natural flexibility and springiness, and traditionally was used for carriage making. The high density of *maple* makes it ideal for hardwearing applications, notably chopping boards and butcher's blocks. *Oak* is uniquely impervious to water, but can be softened with steam and bent into shape. It was widely used for boatbuilding.

*Above* An elegant bureau designed by Tony McMullen, using a mixture of solid wood and veneers in contrasting colours.

*Above* Mapa stacking dining chair by the vk&c partnership. The design benefits from the contrast between native cherry and sycamore.

### Ergonomics

Whatever the appearance of a piece of furniture, certain principles should be carefully observed to ensure that it performs its function correctly. A chair that is impossible to sit on comfortably could be said to have failed as a chair, no matter how striking, inventive or original the design.

A desk or workstation at the wrong height may encourage an unhealthy posture and you could easily do yourself harm without realizing it. By maintaining certain basic dimensional relationships when making furniture, you can still develop original designs while making sure that form and function work together to make a well-balanced product.

Therefore, good woodworking design is achieved by combining well-established principles with a feel for the potential of the material. The colour and figure of different types of wood are so variable that there is no limit to the effects that can be achieved. Even so-called defects in the grain can be displayed to advantage by emphasizing the natural qualities of the wood.

Choosing the finish can make a difference to the design – a high gloss will scatter light and add depth and colour, but also it can seem cold or formal in the wrong context. A simple wax finish generally adds warmth and lustre, which grows deeper with every new coat. Although the natural colour of wood is highly regarded, the creative use of stains or coloured polish can produce unusual and quite striking results.

Good contrasts can be obtained by working with light and dark woods. For example, a light wood interior will "expand" the space inside a cabinet and dark wooden legs on a light coloured table top will give it a more solid appearance.

**Chair to table height**

750mm (30in)

Typing position

Angled chair back

700mm (27½in)

720–750mm (28–30in)

650mm (25½in) legroom

80–85°

400–450mm (16–18in)

450mm (18in)

350mm (14in) seat depth

# CONSTRUCTION TIPS

No matter how creative your design, it is sensible to observe sound
construction principles to make your work safe to use and give it a long life.
Some of these are common sense; others have been developed from years of
experience. Depart from traditional techniques by all means, but not without
considering their purpose.

## Strengthening a shelf

The shape and size of a storage cupboard or bookshelf
should not encourage overloading. Strengthen shelves by
adding a length of rebated (rabbeted) moulding along the
front edge.

## Fittings for safety

Fall flap stay

Fall flap

Choose the correct fittings so that moving parts do not
open too far and strain the hinges or cause injury. A fall
flap stay allows the flap of a bureau, or the lid of a box, to
fold out and come to rest in the right position.

## Stiffening corners

Stiffening members can be added, concealed if necessary,
to hold a wooden frame square and prevent the joints from
working loose. In a wall cupboard, even two relatively thin
strips across the back will stiffen the structure without the
need for a solid back panel.

## Using knock-down fittings

Corner leg
connector

Steel angle plates or brackets, or knock-down fittings, can
be used to strengthen joints, as well as allowing a piece
to be taken apart if required. These ingenious corner
brackets are used to fix the detachable legs and connect
the side rails at the same time.

## Movement

Even well-seasoned wood is prone to movement under different conditions of humidity and temperature. Understanding the behaviour of wood helps in developing construction methods to allow for its natural tendency to move. Even though modern adhesives are much more permanent than those used previously, they will not prevent wood from swelling or splitting.

A moisture-resistant finish coat may help to stabilize a piece, but as soon as the film is penetrated, it can lift or craze. In earlier times, woodworkers understood this and designed furniture to allow for natural movement.

Tongued, grooved and beaded panel

It is better not to fix panelling into its surrounding frame, but allow it to move naturally within a groove. The beaded edge on a tongued-and-grooved moulding is not merely decorative – it creates a shadow line to distract the eye from the gap caused by natural shrinkage.

## Gluing boards

When several boards are glued together on edge, the direction of the growth rings should be alternated to counteract the "cupping" tendency of the wood. Quarter-sawn boards, with the rings running at right angles to the surface, are much more stable in this respect.

Growth rings in same direction – will lead to cupping.

Alternate growth rings on plain-sawn boards minimize distortion

Quarter-sawn boards

## Table top fixing

Expansion plate

Button

A table top can be fixed with shrinkage plates, or small wooden blocks known as buttons. These are slotted into a groove to accommodate the greater movement of the wide boards relative to the narrow members of the supporting frame.

## Finishing

Safety principles should also be observed when selecting the finish for your work. Never use oil-based paints or varnishes on toys or children's furniture – acrylic-based stains and coatings are non-toxic and safe. Oiled wood is heat-resistant, but modern finishing oils contain mineral extracts and should not be used on items that come into contact with food, such as bowls and countertops.

French polish provides a high-quality finish, but is not heat-resistant and will soften on contact with alcohol, so it is not always the ideal choice for a table top.

# FIXINGS AND FITTINGS

**F**ixings and fastenings, or hardware, play an important part in almost every wood project, and it is worth getting to grips with the different types to be able to choose the most suitable. There is a wide range of sizes and patterns, but each has been devised and developed over the years to meet a specific need. Nails and screws, whether designed for mechanical strength or more decorative qualities, can make all the difference to a job when used correctly.

In the same way, the choice of hardware fittings is so vast that you are certain to find the right item to complete a project. Some have a purely functional purpose, while others are more decorative. A pair of well-designed brass hinges, for example, has both qualities and can really add the finishing touch to a well-made piece of work.

# SCREWS AND NAILS

Given the many types of nail, pin and screw that are manufactured, you can be sure that there will be one to suit any application. Inevitably, over time, you will build up a huge collection of fixings (hardware), and it is always worth the effort to keep them sorted into different sizes and types ready for use. Nothing is more frustrating than to reach the assembly stage of a piece of work and find you cannot complete it for the lack of the right size of screw and nail. It is very easy to ruin the work by making do with something fairly close, but if it is a little too long or too wide, it can easily split the wood. Use small jars or tins to store different types, sorting them by size and length, and labelling them so that they are easily identified.

## Screws

These provide a more positive fixing than nails and generally are more useful for strong construction work. The size of the screw is determined by the size of the shank or the diameter of the gauge, and is denoted numerically. A No. 4 gauge is slightly smaller than 3mm (⅛in) in diameter and about the smallest size in common use; a No. 12 is 6mm (¼in) in diameter and used for heavy-duty constructional work. The gauge of the screw does not change with the length of the screw.

In general, the smaller the gauge, the shorter the range of lengths that will be available. For general cabinet work, a No. 8 screw is a convenient size, and is available in lengths from 19–75mm (¾–3in).

Regardless of size, all screws should be long enough to pass through the piece to be secured and penetrate approximately three-quarters of the depth of the second component. If there are lots of screwholes in a piece, wrap a piece of tape around the bit to mark the depth on the bit.

**Wood screw** The standard traditional wood screw, with a single slotted head and tapered shank. It requires a clearance hole of the correct size, counter-sunk to accommodate the head. It is the cheapest type of general-purpose screw and it is made in mild steel with a "self colour" finish. This means that the steel is untreated and will corrode easily in damp conditions.

**Roundhead screws** These are intended to be seen; the flat underside of the head provides extra grip.

**Raised and countersunk wood screw** This has a shallow domed head, which projects slightly above the surface and looks quite decorative.

**Pozidriv head** This is a more modern and very popular form of wood screw with a cross-head for extra grip. It is countersunk with a cross-head slot and zinc plated for rust-resistance. The shank is parallel, rather than tapered, making it suitable for driving into manufactured boards, using a suitably sized pilot hole, without splitting. Made of hardened steel, it is suitable for use with a powered screwdriver.

**Black japanned roundhead screws** are commonly used with black iron fittings for decorative purposes.

**Brass screws** These are less strong than steel screws of the same gauge, but have the great advantage that they will not rust or bind in the wood. Brass countersunk wood screws are perfectly acceptable in cabinet-making. They look neat when they are sunk flush with the surface. In hardwood, first drive in a steel screw of the same size as the brass screw, and then drive in the brass one.

**Surface screws** Modern furniture is frequently assembled using these, with the heads being concealed by plastic caps. These allow the unit to be taken apart if required. Each small plastic cap clips on to a washer under the screwhead. Different colours are available to suit the material's finish.

**Brass cup and washer** This is a more decorative version of the screw cap. It is designed for use with a brass countersunk screw and is ideal for fixing removable panels, such as bath panels. Screw cups and washers spread the pressure of the screw.

**Security screws** have shaped heads, allowing them to be inserted with a flat-bladed screwdriver, but making removal impossible. The slot in the screw head is shaped so that the screwdriver will only grip when turned clockwise.

**Mirror screw and cups** This has a chrome-plated cap that screws over the head after fixing it. Domed (top) and flat versions are available as above.

**Recessed cup washer** Available for recessing into the wood. Drill a counterbore of the correct size to sink the cup flush with the surface.

Nail set
(punch)

## Nails and pins

By far the most common type is the standard wire nail, which is available from 19–150mm (¾–6in) in length. These are fine for structural work, but are best used where they will be concealed, as the heads are difficult to sink down below the surface of the wood without causing it to split.

Lost head nails solve this problem. As their name implies, they can be set just flush with the surface and filled in if necessary. They are ideal for nailing battens (cleats) down and some larger components.

Oval nails have an oval section throughout their length, making them less likely to split the wood.

Annular, or ring, nails have small rings or grooves formed in the shank in order to grip the wood. They are ideal for permanent attachments, as they are difficult to remove.

Panel pins (brads) come into their own for fixing small sizes of wood and delicate mouldings.

Brass panel pins will not rust or cause stains and can be left with their heads showing if desired.

Carpet tacks have wide, flat heads and are made of hardened steel.

Upholstery pins provide a decorative means of securing upholstery work and have wide, flat-bottomed heads so that they grip the fabric.

When working with small sections of timber, or particularly brittle components, it is worth drilling small pilot holes for fixings to prevent the wood from splitting. Use a cross pein or pin hammer for delicate work, and leave the head of each nail protruding just above the surface.

To punch, or "set", the nail head below the surface of the wood, use a nail set, which has a small-cupped end to fit over the head and punch a neat hole in the wood. Nail sets are available in a range of sizes to suit different nails. The resulting hole can be filled with a coloured stopping for an undetectable fixing.

## Varieties of nails and pins

Wire nail

Lost head nail

Oval nail

Wire nail

Annular, or ring, nail

Panel pin (brad)

Brass panel pin

Carpet tack

Upholstery pin

# ASSEMBLY FITTINGS AND HINGES

The introduction of modern flat-pack furniture has generated a large range of custom-made assembly fittings, sometimes called knock-down or K-D fittings, which enable the home user to assemble and dismantle them without special tools. They are equally useful for making your own furniture, as they provide very rigid joints. All that is required is some care in drilling the correct locating holes. K-D fittings are obtainable from many good hardware stores, do-it-yourself stores and mail-order suppliers.

**Brass guide dowel** Used in conjunction with a cross-dowel to ensure perfect alignment as the joint is pulled up tight, preventing it from twisting. Guide dowels are equally useful for lining up the leaves of a table or an inserted panel.

**Panel connector** A device for connecting two panels side by side, as in a row of fitted base units. Also known as a *barrel nut* or *sleeve nut*. The bolt screws into the sleeved connector, clamping the units together and providing lateral location.

**Expansion, or shrinkage, plate** This angled bracket is ideal for attaching a table top or countertop made of solid boards. The slotted screw holes in the upper flange allow the top to expand or shrink slightly without becoming loose. It is also useful for attaching any kind of panel or fascia, and allows for accurate alignment.

**Corner bracket** Ideal for attaching a work surface or table top, it holds the corners of the framework square at the same time.

**Cam fitting** This ingenious cam fitting allows two panels to be joined at a right angle. A quarter turn of the integral screw tightens it against a cam, drawing the two components together. They can be disconnected easily when required.

**Worktop connector** Sometimes called a handrail connector. It uses a positive bolt action to draw two components tightly together.

**Corner bracket** This is designed for attaching table legs and strengthening the corner joints at the same time. The two lugs on the bracket locate into slots in the rails of the table and lock them together as the central bolt is tightened into the leg.

**Countertop connector** When attaching countertops made of chipboard and other man-made boards, expansion plates are not required as the materials are stable. These connector blocks are fitted into holes drilled inside the top edge of a cabinet and have holes for the screws. The holes are angled to allow easy access for a screwdriver.

**Confirmat screw** Designed for fixing into the edge of chipboard without splitting the material. A pilot hole of the exact size removes the chipboard core, and the parallel thread grips the chipboard fibres without expanding the board.

**Cross-dowel connectors** The small steel dowel, threaded to receive the bolt, is inserted into a hole drilled in the face of a panel. The bolt that connects the second component, passes through a hole drilled in the edge of the first panel that intercepts the dowel hole. The recessed bolt provides a strong, square connection.

**T-nut** This is tapped into the reverse side of a panel. A T-nut acts as a captive nut when access is restricted.

## Hinges

Any device that includes a pivot action can be called a hinge, and there are many different variations. Some are designed to be concealed within the framework of a cabinet, or the carcass, while others are intended as decorative features in their own right.

It is important to choose hinges of the correct size and robustness when hanging a door so that it is well supported when it swings open. If a hinge or hinge pin is strained in any way, the door will not fit in the frame and may become detached, causing injury.

## Fitting hinges

Attaching small hinges to cabinet doors requires patience. The style of door will determine the type of hinge required.

Doors which overlap the front of the cabinet can be fitted with butt hinges screwed to the front of the frame, or concealed hinges which are invisible when the door is closed.

Flush doors, which fit inside the cabinet frame, are normally fitted with butt hinges. They need to be recessed into the wood. Mark around the leaf of the hinge with a craft knife or sharp pencil, and form a recess with a chisel.

Flush hinges have very thin leaves, which avoid the need to cut a recess. They are small enough to fit into the small clearance gap surrounding the door.

**Concealed hinge** Originally designed for use in self-assembly base units, this hinge is concealed from view when the door is closed. It clips on to the base plate, allowing the door to be removed easily, and is adjustable in all three directions. A mounting hole is required, using a boring bit to suit the hinge boss.

**Cylinder hinge** Even more discreet, the barrel of the cylinder hinge is concealed in the edges of the door and frame, and is almost invisible when the door is opened. This is only suitable for light-duty use.

**Counter hinges** These are decorative brass hinges, suitable for bar flaps, counter tops and table leaves. Double hinge pins allow the hinge to fold back on itself without binding.

**Lay-on hinge** This is also a concealed hinge, but it requires no mounting holes. It is laid on the surface of the door and frame, and simply screwed in place. The linked pivot arms allow 180 degree opening and are spring-loaded for a positive closing action.

**Pivot hinge** A very discreet and neat hinge, suitable for small cabinet doors. One half screws directly into the frame; the matching half (not shown) screws into the edge of the door and slips over the brass pin of the former, allowing the door to be lifted on and off.

**Lift-off hinge** A decorative hinge in polished brass with finials at the ends, which can be separated, allowing the door to be lifted on and off at will.

**Flush hinges** The slimline design of these hinges allows them to be fitted without the need for chiselled recesses. One leaf folds inside the other to provide a very neat connection.

**Butt hinges** The classic hinge style that is machined from solid brass for a smooth action. It requires a recess chiselled in both door and frame. Butt hinges are available in sizes from as small as 12mm (½in), for use in a jewellery box for example, up to 100mm (4in) for hanging full-size doors.

**Piano hinge** A continuous brass-strip hinge, sold in lengths up to 1.8m (6ft) and having all kinds of use. It is ideal for fitting a lid to a box or, indeed, a lid to a piano.

# STAYS, CATCHES AND DOOR FITTINGS

You should consider buying these fittings in advance. They are an important part of making and designing furniture and especially in the case of door and drawer handles, they will add the finishing touches to your design. There are many specialist outlets that sell all manner of stays, catches and door fittings and most can be ordered by mail order. The style and size of fittings should be chosen with some care to suit the overall design.

**Shelf support**
A small torpedo-shaped shelf support that fits into a 5mm (³⁄₁₆in) hole in the side of a cabinet, making a very unobtrusive fitting.

## Stays and catches

Features such as nylon bearings and spring-loaded magnets make all kinds of ingenious fitting possible, expanding the range of hardware available to the cabinet-maker. For example, they can be used to design a cabinet door that springs open with a slight touch, requiring no handles at all. If you intend using any of these devices, it is advisable to obtain a sample first and study its operation before building the project. Although any hardware may be the last item to be installed, it must be included in your plans at the design stage.

**Drawer runners** Epoxy-coated drawer runners with nylon bearings make sticking drawers things of the past. In left- and right-handed pairs, these runners are available in various lengths to suit different sizes of drawer, but are a consistent 12.5mm (½in) wide when assembled. Therefore, a drawer box should be made exactly 25mm (1in) smaller than the internal size of the cabinet or cupboard.

**Flap stay** A reasonably heavy-duty, long-throw, solid brass flap stay, suitable for vertical and horizontal flaps, with self-lubricating nylon glide bearing. Reversible for fitting to the left- or right-hand end of a unit.

**Glass shelf support** A small shelf support made of transparent plastic so that it is hardly visible. Incorporates a safety catch to prevent the shelf from being knocked accidentally out of place.

**Lid stay** A light-duty stay for less demanding operations, and only in plated brass. There are many varieties of lid and flap stay available to suit a wide range of applications.

## Brass shelf support

Small brass clips that fit into a slotted bookcase strip, allowing shelves to be positioned at will.

## Magnetic touch latch

This latch is spring-loaded so that a light touch on the closed door will release it and throw it open. To close the door, gently push it until the keeper plate and latch connect, and it clicks shut.

**Bed fitting** Used for connecting two panels at a right angle, such as the end and side panels of a small bed or cot. Screw one half to each panel, slot together and they interlock with a tapering fit. However, they can be detached easily when required.

**Keeper plate**
Used with a furniture bolt.

**Miniature magnetic catch**
A very discreet catch, suitable for small cabinet doors. The barrel containing the magnet is recessed into the door frame, while the tiny striking plate is simply tapped into the door like a drawing pin (thumb tack).

**Keeper plate**
Used with an auto latch.

**Furniture bolt** Unlike a barrel bolt, a furniture bolt has a flat profile and is much less obtrusive. It is spring-loaded to prevent it from rattling.

## Door fittings

Whether the style of your project is traditional or ultra-modern, there is sure to be a range of door hardware to suit. Cabinet doors can be fitted with a variety of handles and knobs. Often, changing the handles can improve the appearance of a cabinet considerably.

For a set of doors or drawers, you can fit knobs or drop handles ranging from a reproduction style in Florentine bronze to slimline chrome or satin aluminium. Natural wood, ready for staining and polishing, or ceramic knobs to match a painted finish are other options. The size of fittings should be chosen with care to suit the overall proportions of the design.

**Door handles** D-shaped handles in oak and pine, can be unfinished for staining or polishing to match the finish of the unit. A recessed oak handle, for flat mounting to a door or drawer front, provides a finger pull with no holes required.

**Escutcheon** A key hole can be covered with an escutcheon plate, or a discreet insert can be pushed into the hole, protecting it from wear.

**Fall-flap lock** This type of lock is designed for the fall flap of a bureau or cocktail cabinet and has a special security feature: the key can only be removed when the flap is locked shut.

**Auto door latch** A spring-loaded door latch that allows a cabinet door to be closed or sprung open by gentle pressure, so you do not need a handle.

**Wooden door knobs**
Turned knobs in oak, beech and pine, a few examples of the different sizes and styles available. Although these are sanded ready for finishing, they can also be obtained ready-lacquered.

**Cabinet locks** A rim lock fits on the inside of a cabinet door or flap, mounted on the surface. A mortise lock is neater and more secure, and is inserted into a mortise cut in the edge of the door.

**Reproduction handles**
A wide range of pull handles is made for reproduction furniture, offering different decorative styles with interchangeable base plates. These items are made with a copper, brass, bronze or pewter finish.

**Magnetic door catch**
A simple device, with a small keeper plate that is screwed to the inside of a door. The magnet in the body of the catch keeps the door closed.

**Ceramic knobs**
White, cream and decorated ceramic knobs are made in a range of sizes and look good on painted furniture.

**Satin aluminium knob**
Metallic knobs give a contemporary look. They may be made in aluminium, steel or brass, with a highly polished, brushed, chromed, satin or even gold-plated finish.

**Shell handle** Typical of Shaker-style furniture, this nickel-plated handle is suitable as a drawer pull.

# BASIC TECHNIQUES

**5**

**S**tudy the finest example of cabinet-making, and no matter how complex it may seem, you can be sure of one thing: when it was made, the same skills were used as in the simplest of projects. Selecting wood and cutting it to size, shaping the individual components, assembling and gluing them together, then sanding and preparing for a final finish – all woodworking, at all levels, depends on these elementary principles. To develop your ability from novice to expert requires time, patience and application: persevere until experience begins to make the difference.

There are no easy short-cuts, but in the following pages you will find plenty of advice that will help you achieve your goals. An understanding of how hand and power tools work, and how wood behaves, will provide a good grounding for improving your skills and expertise.

# MEASURING AND MARKING

There is a saying often repeated in woodworking: "Measure twice and cut once." It may seem obvious advice, but when woodworkers repeat it, you can be sure that they speak from experience – there is not a woodworker in the world who does not occasionally forget this basic rule. By adopting a simple discipline for measuring and marking out, you can reduce the risk of making mistakes in your work. Before even laying hands on your tools, check and double check. The simplest of errors can produce the most costly results.

### Measuring tapes

A retractable measuring tape is a basic essential. Choose one with a lockable blade and clear markings – the quality can vary considerably. A double scale showing both imperial and metric measurements can be useful, allowing quick conversion across the scales.

Inspect the hooked end of the tape measure regularly for wear – this is a common cause of inaccuracy, so try not to let the tape spring back into its casing out of control, which could damage the end. The retracting spring in the centre of the tape will lose its effectiveness if fully extended, so if you find this occurring regularly, you should consider buying a longer rule. A 3m (10ft) or 5m (16ft) rule should be adequate for most workshop tasks.

It is a good idea to lubricate and clean the blade from time to time by applying a drop of oil with a soft cloth as the blade is retracted.

Top

Marking rod

**Marking rods**

Shoulder line

*Above* Use a combination square as a try square or as a normal rule.

### Steel rules

A fixed steel rule with a permanently engraved scale will be better than a retractable tape where accuracy is required, such as when setting out joints and fine detail. A combination square is even more useful – it combines a steel rule with a sliding stock that acts as a try square and adjustable gauge all in one. If there are curves, you will achieve greater accuracy with a flexible steel rule.

### Marking divisions

To divide the width of a board in half, or into any number of equal strips, you can save calculation and the risk of error with this quick method. Lay a steel rule at a 45 degree angle across the work with an even number of divisions from edge to edge. Simply use the scale to mark off the intervals you need; repeat at the other end of the board, and join the marks with a straightedge or chalk line.

### Marking rods

When marking out a number of identical components, use a marking rod to reduce measuring errors. This is a straight length of square batten with suitable reference points marked on it. It is a simple matter to set out all the details of complex joinery on this master pattern without discrepancy. Keep it safe as a permanent record of each job you do – you never know when it might be useful again.

## Face and edge marks

Wood is an organic material and by its nature will be subject to variations in size, even after it has been cut from the tree. Woodworkers deal with this by always using one edge as a basis for all their measurements and setting out. Establish a procedure for marking up your work and follow it every time until it becomes second nature.

Select every component individually, bearing in mind its position in the construction. Grain

pattern and direction, possible shrinkage, how much it will be seen, how it will be finished, and the strength and design of any joints required are all factors that should influence your decision in selecting the "face side" of any piece of wood. This attention to detail is the secret of quality woodwork. True-up (square) the face of the wood with a try plane or jack plane. The surface must not only be straight, but free of any "wind" or twist between opposite corners.

1 On a wide piece of wood, use a pair of winding rods – place a straightedge at one end of the board and sight across it to another at the far end.

2 Use a try square or a combination square to check that one long edge is square to the face. Place the stock of the square against the face edge, with the blade on the face side.

When using a try square to check if the edge is square, sight along the surface toward a light source and slide the square from one end of the wood to the other – any small gaps will be visible. Adjust with the plane if necessary and mark the wood as shown where the two faces meet. Take all your measurements from the face edge/face side and you will eliminate any discrepancies in width or depth that might affect the overall dimensions of the finished piece.

### Face and edge marks

Try square      Face side

Face edge      Face mark

## Marking and mortise gauges

A marking gauge has a single point and adjustable stock, and is used for scribing a line at a fixed distance from an edge; a mortise gauge (left) has two adjustable points, allowing parallel lines to be scribed.

To set up the mortise gauge, adjust the points and slide the stock to approximately the correct position, then turn the locking screw of the stock until it just "nips" on to the beam. Gently tap one end of the beam against the bench to make fine adjustments before finally tightening the screw. When gauging lines on timber (lumber), always run the stock of the gauge along the face side and edge. Set the points to the width of the chisel you intend to use to cut the mortise, not from a rule.

## Scribing

When setting out lines for cutting or making joints, score across the grain of the timber with a bradawl (awl) or sharp knife. This prevents the wood fibres from tearing out along the grain, and provides an accurate guide when paring down to the line with a chisel or plane for a final fit.

# USING HAND SAWS

Cutting the material to size is the first stage of any project, and without doubt
the art of sawing straight and true is the first vital skill to acquire. You should
persevere with the correct technique until it becomes instinctive.
Understanding how a saw works, and how the wood behaves as it is cut, is the
key. If the teeth lose their cutting edge, or the set of the teeth becomes uneven
through constant use, you will find it impossible to saw straight.

### Sawing technique

Hand saws come in many types and
sizes. An all-purpose panel saw and a
good-quality tenon saw are the two
basics to get you started. As your
technique improves, and you explore
the different demands of woodworking
and the different properties of
hardwoods, softwoods and sheet
materials, you will soon find your
collection of saws expanding.
Nevertheless, the essential technique
remains the same.

First of all, clamp the wood firmly
to the bench. Forgetting this simple
step is the most common cause of
accidents – sawing accurately requires
both hands for good balance, even
though a hand saw looks like a one-
handed tool.

Position yourself squarely over the
piece, with your line of sight directly
above the cutting line. Always make
sure the saw cuts just to the waste side
of the line to allow for the width of
the cut, or kerf.

Start the cut slowly and form a
groove. Some saws have a group of
finer teeth at the tip of the blade for
this very purpose. Hold the blade at a
steep angle, sighting down and over
the edge of the work to keep the cut
absolutely square and vertical. This
first step guides the saw for the rest of
the cutting action.

Gradually decrease the angle of the
cut and lengthen the strokes of the
saw blade. Allow the blade to do the

work – do not force it through the
wood. You will learn what it means to
hear a good sharp hand saw "singing"
as it cuts rhythmically. Use all your arm
to generate the sawing action, keeping
the upper arm, elbow and wrist in
line; use your forefinger to direct and
steady the saw. When cutting large
boards, arrange a support to take the
weight of the scrap, but make sure it
does not force the work upwards and
cause the saw blade to bind in the cut.

**1** Start the cut very slowly with the
tip of the saw blade, drawing it
back and forth to form a groove, and
guiding it with your thumb.

**2** As you near the end of the cut,
support the waste with your other
hand and use shorter, gentler strokes
to sever the last few fibres.

| Ripsaw | Crosscut saw | Fleam cut saw |
|---|---|---|
| Use this for cutting along the grain of wood with a ripping action. The teeth are coarse set with a deep gullet to clear the waste quickly and prevent the saw from binding, particularly in resinous softwoods. The size and spacing of the teeth are specified as Teeth per Inch (TPI) – very coarse ripsaws can have as few as four or five TPI. | A crosscut saw is designed for cutting across the grain of timber. Each tooth is sharpened at an angle to the grain to prevent it from tearing. The teeth are smaller and finer than those of a ripsaw, up to 12–13 TPI. | Many modern saws are made with dual-purpose teeth for general use. The teeth are specially hardened and ideal for cutting sheet materials, but they cannot be resharpened. |

90°

TPI    Gullet

65°

Set

45°

## Tenon saws

Sometimes called backsaws, tenon saws produce a finer cut for joinery work. A stiff spine along the top of the blade keeps it straight and adds weight to the saw. This weight will cause it to find its own way through the work as you guide it.

When cutting end grain, turn it around for the second cut so that the waste is always on the same side of the saw blade.

1 Make a small nick in the wood at an angle to start off the saw cut. Sight down the line to establish a good square cut. Concentrate on the direction of the saw.

2 Slowly increase the length of your stroke and lower the saw with each cut until it is completely horizontal to the wood. Do not grip the saw too tightly.

3 To make cuts in the end grain, clamp the work or piece of wood upright in a vice and saw down to the shoulder line, stopping exactly at the line.

## Mitre saws

For cutting very fine mouldings and angles, this relatively new type of saw will soon repay its modest investment, especially if you intend to do a lot of framing work. The wide tensioned blade with specially hardened teeth slides within its own carriage, which can be set to any angle between 45 and 90 degrees.

1 Hold or clamp the wood firmly against the backstop and work the blade back and forth with a smooth cutting action. Very little downward force is required, as the saw operates under its own weight and has its own guide mechanism. Always cut on the waste side of the marked line for perfect results.

## Sharpening saws

A good-quality hand saw will last for years if looked after well; indeed, many woodworkers will say that a saw improves with age. If it needs sharpening, check the set of the teeth first. Each tooth on a saw is a miniature cutting blade that slices through the wood and clears a path for the next one. The teeth are "set" (angled) alternately to each side to prevent the saw blade from binding in the work.

When using a saw file, work systematically along the saw, sharpening each alternate tooth, then work from the other side to complete the process.

1 To reset a saw, clamp the blade between two strips of wood to protect and support it. Adjust the gauge of the saw setting tool to suit the number of teeth per inch, and work down the blade, applying the correct amount of set to each alternate tooth in turn.

2 A saw file is a triangular file with a sliding carriage that fits over the top of the blade. Set the carriage to suit the cutting angle of the teeth, settle the file in the gullet, and slowly draw it back and forth a few times until you see bright steel on the face of the tooth.

# USING POWER SAWS

**Portable power saws come into their own when cutting large quantities of wood, especially sheet materials, but they may not be as accurate as hand tools for fine work. Most woodworkers will employ a combination of both to suit each job. As always, follow the manufacturer's guidance for their safe use, and always fit sharp blades. It is false economy, and very dangerous, to work with a cutting tool unless it is set up properly and working efficiently.**

### Circular saws

Choose a model with the motor power and type of blade to suit the work. For cutting most sheet materials up to 19mm (¾in) thick, a 1,000W motor and tungsten-carbide-tipped blade, with a diameter of 165–180mm (6½–7in), will be adequate. Heavier work, especially in hardwood,

requires a more powerful motor and a greater depth of cut. You will soon burn out the motor if you overload it. Make sure that the spring-loaded safety guard is in working order, and regularly clear it of sawdust as you work. Make a habit of checking the power cord after every use, and attend to any signs of wear immediately.

With practice, you will be able to cut straight lines freehand, but using a guide is safer and more accurate. An adjustable fence is often supplied, but this will be useful for cutting strips only up to about 150mm (6in) wide. For larger sizes, pin a straight-edged batten to the wood as a guide for the saw's sole plate.

### Cutting straight stock from a board

1 Make sure the power saw is disconnected from the power supply, then measure the distance from the edge of the base plate to the blade. To be absolutely accurate when cutting, you should allow for the extra thickness of the tungsten-carbide tips on the blade.

2 Mark the distance away from the cutting line and draw a parallel line along the work. Pin or clamp a straight-edge along this line, then run the sole plate of the saw along it. In some cases, the body of the saw will overhang the base plate, so choose a batten thickness that will not obstruct the saw.

3 Fit the parallel fence to the base plate and saw back in the other direction to reduce the board to the correct width. Make sure it is clamped firmly to the bench. A circular saw will make light work of cutting wood, but be sure not to overload it, and always have the guards in place.

### Making a circular saw jig

If you want to cut large quantities of sheet material, make up a simple sawing jig for quickly setting out square cuts.

Cut two strips of 12mm (½in) plywood as shown and assemble them to form a table on which the circular saw's base plate can travel. Set the upper strip back from the cutting edge by the exact width of the base plate to the left of the saw blade. Fix a cross-batten square across the bottom of the jig. Now place the jig on the panel of sheet material, line it up with the cutting line and run the saw along the line.

Width of base plate to saw blade

Cut line

## Jigsaws

A jigsaw is one of the most versatile cutting tools you can have in the workshop, being suitable for both straight and curved cuts.

It has a small, reciprocating and narrow blade. It is hand held and easy to use without much setting up. As it is so portable, take particular care to keep the power cord out of the way when working.

If possible, buy a model with a pendulum blade action – this clears the sawdust better and makes a straighter cut in wood. Electronic speed control allows you to slow the cutting action for very delicate work. The variety of jigsaw blades available makes this tool useful for cutting many sheet materials into smaller pieces, including thin sheet metal.

1 Because the jigsaw blade cuts on the upward stroke, there is a much greater risk of splintering the wood, particularly when cutting across the grain. When working with veneered panels, score along the cut line with a knife and cut just outside the line, then pare down to the cut line with a plane.

2 An alternative is to fit a small, transparent shoe that clips around the blade and presses down on to the surface directly in front of it to keep breakout to a minimum.

3 A useful accessory with some machines is a plastic cover that fits over the sole plate to protect delicate surfaces. If you find that the sole plate is bruising the wood surface too easily, you are probably forcing the saw too much – use a slower speed or fit a new, sharp blade.

## Crosscut saws

Powered crosscut saws, also called mitre saws or "snip-off" saws, make accurate crosscutting of timber (lumber) a simple matter. The best models extend to a capacity of 250mm (10in), allowing extra wide boards to be cut.

Note that the blades are not interchangeable with other circular saws – the plunging action of the saw requires a different tooth profile. It is best to check what type of blades you'll need by reading the manufacturer's instructions.

1 The saw body can be adjusted to any angle, and a compound mitre saw, as shown, will cut two angles simultaneously. It is ideal for framing work and cutting mouldings and coving sections.

2 To save time when making a number of identical components for a piece of work, establish the correct size for the first one. Then clamp a small spacing block to the table to save marking up the rest.

# USING CHISELS

**Always aim to remove as much excess wood as possible from the cut before using your chisel. For example, remove the wood with a saw before cleaning up with a chisel or, when cutting a mortise, drill out as much of the waste as possible and use the chisel to clean and square-up the sides.**

### Chisels

There are two principal types of chisel used for general woodworking and cabinet-making: firmer and bevelled, or bevel-edged. A firmer chisel, with a stout blade and heavy-duty handle designed to accept blows from a mallet, is used for making mortises by chopping down across the tougher end grain of wood. Bevelled chisels may be more familiar, and they have many more uses. The bevelled tip of the blade is weaker and will not stand up to continuous heavy use, but it will suffice for most medium-duty work. This type of chisel comes into its own when used by hand alone for removing small amounts of wood with a gentle paring action.

### Care of chisels

Chisels should always be kept sharp – they can slip away from the work and cause a lot of damage as soon as they lose their edge. Make a habit of sharpening them at the end of every work session (in the same manner as plane blades), and store them safely, either in a box or in a wall-mounted rack that protects the tips. A well-maintained set of chisels should last a lifetime.

1 Scribe the width of the mortise with a mortise gauge and cut across the grain at each end to prevent breakout. Use the firmer chisel, almost vertical with the bevel down, to make a series of deep cuts. Start at the middle and work toward one end, then reverse the chisel for the other end. Clear out any waste as you work – large, wedge-shaped chunks of wood can be chopped out quite easily.

2 When you have reached sufficient depth, place the chisel at the very end of the mortise with the bevel facing inward. Strike sharply with the mallet to plunge the blade vertically down and form a good square corner. Push the chisel blade slowly forward to disengage it and true-up (square) the sides at the same time.

3 To clean up the shoulder of a joint, hold the chisel vertical and steady the blade with your other hand. Lean over it and slice down for a clean cut.

### Tip

Do not leave chisels lying on a bench where the blades can come into contact with metal objects. Fit them with plastic blade guards or keep them in a chisel roll.

4 In the absence of a shoulder plane, a bevelled chisel can be used to pare across the grain of a tenon joint. Use the widest chisel available, and hold it perfectly flat so that it slides evenly over the surface of the wood, removing the minimum amount with each stroke. A paring chisel has an even longer blade and is ideal for this kind of finishing work, but it should never be struck with a mallet.

# USING PLANES

A woodworker will build a collection of planes over time, each having a different use. Planes should have a good-quality "iron" (blade), made of tool steel with a bevelled edge for removing fine shavings of wood. Good-quality planes are sufficiently weighty to avoid "chatter". The size and shape of the sole, or base, and the angle and adjustment of the iron will determine a plane's best function.

### Jack plane

This is used mainly for dressing large areas of sawn or uneven wood. The sole, at 300–380mm (12–15in) long, acts to even out high spots and ridges as you work. Use with a slicing action, angled slightly across the grain, to make a level surface, then make even strokes along the grain to finish off. The try plane, or jointer plane, is longer – up to 610mm (24in) – and is used to true-up (square) the long straight edges of boards before joining.

### Smoothing plane

Ranging in length from 225 to 265mm (9 to 10½in), the smoothing plane is an all-purpose plane for most general carpentry and joinery work. It is an excellent plane to start your collection with.

### Rebate plane

The rebate, or filister, plane has a cutting blade that extends to the full width of the sole, making square-edged rebates (rabbets) simple to achieve. Adjust the side fence and depth stop to suit the size of rebate, then start the cut at the end of the timber (lumber) farthest from you. As the cutter forms the rebate, gradually increase the length of stroke, using your left hand to support the plane and hold it firmly in position.

### Shoulder plane

This miniature rebate plane is good for fine joinery work, as it cuts at a shallow angle, both across the grain and on end grain. The mouth is adjustable to allow the removal of small slivers of wood when paring down for a final fit.

### Block plane

Use the block plane for all kinds of fine finishing. Its blade is set at a shallow angle, allowing the removal of very fine shavings; the bevel on the blade faces upward, rather than down to the wood surface as in most other planes. It is very controllable, being designed for one-handed use.

A sharp and finely set block plane will remove the end grain quite easily. Make up a simple shooting board, as shown, to square the ends of components before jointing. It hooks over the edge of the bench and provides a firm support for the work, while holding the plane body square. Turn the board over for use as a straightforward bench hook.

### Moulding plane

More often found in antique shops these days, old moulding planes, in good condition, can still be useful. The plane iron is held in a hardwood body by a wooden wedge and tapped into place. As with a rebate plane, start shaping the moulding at the farthest end of the piece and work with increasingly longer strokes as the profile is formed.

# USING POWER PLANERS AND ROUTERS

Power planers are ideal machines for removing large amounts of waste quickly, but they can also be used with some accuracy for fine finishing. Different models on offer vary in size and capacity – look for a minimum depth of cut of 3mm (⅛in) and a dust extraction facility or dust bag to collect the copious shavings produced. Tungsten-carbide-tipped (TCT) disposable blades are best when working with manufactured boards.

### Electric planers

These can be very aggressive when removing stock, so hold the tool with both hands and keep it moving so that it does not cut for too long in one spot. As with the hand tool, an electric planer can also be used across the grain of wide boards for quick results, provided final finishing is with the grain. Although the electric planer is very fast, the hand-held version rarely gives the quality of finish that can be achieved with a well-set and sharpened bench plane. Check for sharpness and adjustment each time an electric planer is used – and make sure the wood to be planed is held firmly in a vice or clamped down.

1 The depth of cut is controlled by the rotary knob at the front, which doubles as a handle. Push down firmly and evenly on the machine to remove a constant thickness of stock in one pass. The side fence keeps the sole plate square to the edge.

2 Most planers have a V-groove machined in the bottom of the sole plate to permit chamfering. Locate the groove on the square edge of the work to position the cutters at 45 degrees to each adjoining face. The work is in a jig to hold it in position.

### Sharpening plane irons

Remove the lever cap from the plane by raising the lever at the top, then take out the blade assembly. Slacken the screw on the cap iron and swivel the plane iron until it can be lifted over the screw head. Do not allow the sharp end of the iron to contact the cap iron body. Apply a coat of thin oil to the oilstone and rest the bevel of the iron on the stone. Rock it up and down until you feel that the bevel is perfectly flat on the stone. Hold the iron at this angle, then slowly slide it backward and forward. Use the forefingers of your other hand to apply pressure evenly over the width of the iron, and move your arms from the elbows, not the wrists.

Check the bevel by turning it face upward – any slight unevenness will indicate that you need to adjust your grip. Increase pressure with even strokes until the whole face of the bevelled edge has been finely ground and you can feel a small burr running evenly along the back edge of the iron. Turn the iron over and press it flat on to the stone. Remove the burr with a few short strokes.

Keep the iron flat – any slight rounding over on the back face will ruin the cutting edge. Wipe off any excess oil and refit the cap iron. Clean any debris from inside the body of the plane before reassembly, and apply a drop of oil to the moving parts of the adjustment mechanism.

3 Some models allow you to form rebates (rabbets) up to 25mm (1in) deep, using the side fence to control the rebate width. The design of the planer body dictates the maximum rebate capacity, so always check this when buying new equipment to ensure that the tool meets your needs.

## Routers

A router is one of the most versatile power tools available to the home woodworker. It uses high-speed rotary cutters, in a variety of profiles, to remove controlled amounts of material with great accuracy. However, certain safety rules should always be observed when operating a router. The router cutter should be presented to the work in the correct direction, so that the cutting edge bites into the wood. If you get this wrong, the cutter will spin out of control and ruin the work. Take the trouble to double check this every time you use the tool by observing the "clockwise" rule: looking down at the router, the cutter will always turn clockwise into the work. Always clamp the work firmly to prevent accidents, and keep the power cord well out of the way by draping it over your shoulder.

Direction of travel

Direction of rotation

Direction of travel

1 Always clamp the work to the bench. Never use the tool single-handed. Grasp it firmly with both hands and push slowly but surely through the wood, letting it cut at its own rate.

2 When using the side fence, a vernier scale allows fine adjustment of the cutter position. It is a good idea to keep plenty of offcuts (scraps) to hand for trial runs to ensure that the router is operating correctly.

3 Do not remove too much waste in one pass – use the adjustable depth stop to lower the cutter into the work in two or three steps. Remove 6–8mm (¼–⅜in) at a time and you will produce a smoother cut.

## Template follower

A template follower allows the repeated production of identical components by following a master pattern. It is particularly useful for creating curved shapes. Disconnect the power cord when making adjustments. Make sure it is completely seated in its recess.

1 Fit the follower attachment to the base of the router using the screws supplied.

2 Measure the distance between the cutting edge of the router bit and the outer rim of the follower. The finished work will exceed the template size by this amount. You must allow for this when constructing the template.

3 A trammel point fitted to the side bars will simplify forming circular shapes to a fixed radius.

Router base

Template

Workpiece

Router bit

Follower

Added edge distance

# USING POWER DRILLS

**Without doubt, a power drill will be one of the most useful tools in your workshop. It is worth investing in a reasonably powerful model, not so much for heavy-duty use, but to guarantee that the motor will last a long time without working at the limit of its capacity.**

### Drill accessories

If your workshop does not have the space to install a free-standing bench (pillar) drill, a vertical drill stand accessory for your standard power drill is well worth considering.

Many drill bits and accessories depend on precise and controlled operation for accuracy and safety.

### Hole-saws

These make short work of cutting large-diameter holes, but they do have to be mounted in a vertical drill stand. Sizes range from 12mm (½in) up to 100mm (4in). Set the drill to a very low speed when drilling large-diameter holes, and clamp down the work securely.

### Spade bits

Also called a flat bit, these are useful for drilling large holes. Before you start drilling, the point of the bit needs to be engaged with the timber (lumber).

1 The traditional spade bit is much safer and more accurate when used in a drill stand. For a neat hole, set the depth stop so that initially the bit sinks just far enough into the wood for the pointed end to pierce the far side and mark the centre of the hole.

2 Turn the work over and use the small hole to centre the spade bit, then complete the hole. In this manner, you will avoid any breakout in the wood.

### Power drill key features:

- Minimum chuck capacity of 10mm (⅜in); ideally 13mm (½in).
- Detachable side handle for extra grip.
- Keyless chuck, allowing the quick change of drill bits with a simple twisting action.
- Variable speed and reversible action for maximum flexibility.
- Lock-on button for continuous running.
- Automatic clutch or torque control, with variable settings, allowing use as a screwdriver.

### Hinge borers

Many furniture fittings are designed to fit in standard hole sizes – for example, concealed cabinet hinges. The two standard sizes are 25mm (1in) and 35mm (1⅜in), and it is worth acquiring the purpose-made hinge boring bits that produce a neat, flat-bottomed blind hole to suit them.

## Sanding accessories

The rotary power of a drill makes it ideal for many sanding and shaping tasks, without using a special tool. Drum sanders use a small sanding belt fitted on a rubber or foam cylinder in various sizes up to 150mm (6in) in diameter. For smoothing curves or cleaning up the edges of a piece of work these small accessories come easily to hand without the cost of a special tool for the same purpose. If using the drill freehand, always fit the side handle to steady the machine, and work against the motion of the rotating drum or disc to give you greater control.

1 Fit a small sanding drum to the drill and pass the work over it, applying gentle pressure. Always wear a dust mask and eye protection when working in this way.

2 You can attach a sanding disc to the drill and use it freehand for shaping curved objects and removing large amounts of surface material extremely quickly.

## Plug cutters

A very useful tool for cabinet-making is the plug cutter. It is fitted into a pillar drill and used to make small wooden pellets or plugs. These are then plugged into holes in the workpiece to conceal fixing screws. Plug cutters are matched to counterbore, or three-in-one, bits in a range of sizes to suit the size of screw, from No. 6 gauge upwards.

1 Use a counterbore or three-in-one drill bit to form the screw hole, sinking the counterbore to a depth of approximately 10mm (⅜in). The tip of the bit, which provides a pilot hole for the screw, is quite fragile, so it is good practice to use a drill stand for this to keep the drill absolutely vertical and avoid breakages.

2 Fit the plug cutter in a drill stand and make a series of small pellets in a matching material. Use stock of suitable thickness (19mm/¾in) and set the cutting depth to about 12mm (½in), leaving all the plugs in place until needed.

3 The easiest way to snap out each pellet is by using a small screwdriver blade or chisel. Apply a drop of wood glue and tap into the screw holes. Match the colour and grain direction of the wood as closely as possible.

4 When the glue is dry and clear, use a very sharp bevelled chisel to pare each pellet flush with the surface of the timber. This will leave it virtually undetectable when finished.

# ASSEMBLY TECHNIQUES

When all the components of your project have been made, you can begin to assemble them. It is always good workshop practice to have a separate area for this operation, so that glued items can be left undisturbed to dry, preferably overnight. A solid bench is essential, and its surface should be perfectly flat. If the assembly bench is warped or uneven, this deformity will be transferred to the item you are making, no matter how accurate the woodwork.

## Drilling

Plan your assembly carefully so that you have enough time to work in stages without rushing the job. A carpenter's brace is a very efficient tool and can sometimes be a quicker option than resorting to a power drill. Auger bits remove large amounts of waste much more accurately in a controlled fashion. Stand directly over the piece of work, using one hand to apply downward force and keep the bit vertical while turning the brace handle with the other hand. Drill pilot holes for any screws, especially in hardwood, countersinking them if required, and clear any debris before fixing the screw.

1 Choose a brace with a ratchet drive if possible, as this will allow you to make half a turn at a time and stand close to the bench.

2 Here a counterbore bit drills a pilot for the screw, a clearance hole for the screw shank, and a recess for the head, all in one operation.

3 Always choose a screwdriver bit to suit the screw heads. Do not allow the screwdriver to slip out of the head and ruin a piece of work.

4 Some cordless drills can be used for inserting screws. You can also obtain purpose-designed electric screwdrivers. An adjustable torque setting ensures that you do not strip the head as the screw is tightened, while a magnetic bit holder saves time when working with steel screws.

## Gluing

Before applying any glue to the assembly, always "dry fit" components together and prepare the work. Always seal glue containers after use to prevent the build-up of dried glue in the nozzle. Modern quick-setting PVA woodworking glue should be applied and clamped tight within ten minutes for the strongest bond. Be warned, however: on fine cabinet work intended for a clear finish, the dissolved glue should not be left to soak into the grain, as it may cause discolouration at the final stage. Sometimes it is advisable to leave the glue to set, then carefully cut away the excess with a sharp blade.

1 Apply PVA woodworking glue evenly to the entire joint surface, using a stiff brush to spread it out.

2 Wipe off any excess glue with a damp cloth as soon as a joint has been assembled and clamped.

## Clamping

Apply pressure to a joint as soon as possible after gluing – make a habit of preparing everything you need in advance. Keep a box of small scraps of wood handy and use them to protect the surface of the work. It is a known fact that you can never have too many clamps, and you will soon start collecting a selection of different types and sizes to suit all kinds of assembly technique.

## Adhesives

The traditional woodworker's adhesive was animal glue. While it has been superseded by more modern glues, it is still obtainable and is useful for restoration work and veneering. Small pearls of the material are melted to form a liquid and brushed on to the wood. Unfortunately, the glue is not heat-resistant and can deteriorate, becoming brittle with time.

For most tasks, the standard adhesive is a quick-setting, water-soluble PVA adhesive or wood glue. Generally creamy white in colour, it becomes transparent when dry, leaving an almost invisible glue line. It is non-toxic, non-flammable, safe to use and easy to remove before it dries with a damp cloth. Wood glue can also be yellow in colour. Rapid-drying and waterproof versions are available.

For heavy-duty applications, or exterior use, a more robust glue is recommended. Two-part adhesives are ideal, hardening by curing chemically. They cannot be dissolved or removed when dry. The glue is mixed by adding a liquid hardener to a powder; only mix a small quantity at a time – sufficient for the job in hand. Resorcinol glue is waterproof and heatproof. It is slightly toxic, so wear gloves to protect your hands when using. Another drawback is that it is a dark reddish brown, which makes it very visible on pale coloured wood.

1 G-clamps come in all sizes, ranging from 25mm (1in) up to 250mm (10in) or more. When buying G-clamps, beware of cheaper types made of low-quality castings – they may shatter as they are tightened. Look for high-grade malleable iron in the specification.

2 Keep a few quick (spring) clamps handy for fast one-handed clamping. They are not suitable for high-pressure applications, but can be useful for fixing complex assemblies temporarily while making final adjustments. Do not be tempted to release clamps too quickly. Allow time for the glue to dry.

3 Use sash (bar) clamps in pairs to apply pressure evenly. They are ideal for assembling doors and panels that require a parallel clamping action to remain square. Think through the sequence for the clamping process and make sure you have enough clamps to hand.

4 Check that a panel is square at the internal corners before applying glue. Accuracy in cutting the shoulders of joints is the key to a square assembly. If the shoulders are slightly out of square, the panel will become permanently deformed when pressure is applied.

### Tip

A good tip for checking the squareness of a panel is to measure the diagonals. If one corner is true, and the diagonals are equal, the panel must be therefore a perfect square or rectangle. Measure both diagonals to make absolutely sure.

# SANDING AND FINISHING

Before applying any finishing coat to your completed work, the wood should be sanded and prepared well. A coat of varnish or polish will show up any blemishes in the surface that were hardly detectable beforehand. Sometimes it is very tempting to rush this part of the process, but there is no substitute for careful and methodical preparation. A power sander will deal with most of the work, but you should always finish off by hand. This gives you the opportunity of checking every part of the assembly and correcting any small defects.

### Using wire wool

Wire, or steel, wool produces an even finer finish than sandpaper. The tiny strands of spun steel fibre burnish the surface of the wood.

The most useful grades range from 0 (coarse) through 00 and 000 to 0000 (very fine). On oily wood, this can leave the surface so smooth that any further finishing is unnecessary. Form a pad from the wire wool when using it, and rub in the direction of the grain. Gently brush along the grain afterwards to remove any fine dust and debris.

1 Form a pad from a small amount of wire (steel) wool and work it along the grain, using smooth, even strokes.

### Using sandpaper

Sandpaper grades are denoted in "grit size". This refers to the size of abrasive particles that are applied in an even coating to the backing paper. Begin with a fairly coarse grade, such as 60 or 80 grit, then use progressively finer grades until the surface is smooth and silky to the touch. Each grade removes the minute scratches left by the previous one. A good range of paper to stock would include 80, 120, 240 and 320 grit for the finest finish; 400 grit is so fine that it is normally used for cutting back the first coat of finish.

1 Use a cork or rubber block on flat surfaces to obtain the right amount of flexibility as you work. You can use a wooden block, but it could tear the sandpaper. Clear the dust away as you work to avoid clogging the paper, particularly on resinous and oily wood.

2 A surform tool is very useful for rounding off the edges of wood, and it is surprisingly accurate. The rows of miniature cutting edges on the blade pare away the surface of the wood with a continuous motion.

3 To finish off a rounded edge, wrap a small square of sandpaper around a section of moulded timber (lumber) of the correct profile (taking care not to tear the sandpaper). Work down through the different grades of sandpaper as normal.

## Using a cabinet scraper

This is a flexible rectangle of high-quality tempered steel, which when used properly makes a versatile cutting tool capable of producing a highly polished finish. Use it before you use abrasive papers, such as garnet paper or silicon carbide, to remove small tears and blemishes.

When you use a cabinet scraper, always with two hands, you should vary the angle of the scraper to fine-tune its cutting action as you push it away from you with smooth strokes.

1 Hold the scraper as shown, flexing the blade between your fingers and thumbs until the cutting edge just begins to bite into the wood surface.

2 You can use other scraper profiles on moulded and curved surfaces, like the gooseneck scraper, which you can turn to suit any concave profile.

## Sharpening a cabinet scraper

A cabinet scraper must be prepared before use and sharpened regularly to maintain its efficiency. The blade is made to scrape rather than cut. The cutting edge must be perfectly flat and square, so it should first be prepared with a file and then polished on an oilstone or grindstone. With the blade fastened in a vice, a hard steel shaft is run along the edge to raise a burr and produce the new cutting edge.

1 The cutting edge of the scraper must be perfectly flat and square before you begin. Clamp it upright in a vice and use a metal file to prepare the edge.

2 Place the edge of the scraper flat on an oilstone and work it back and forth to polish it.

3 Now raise a burr all along the edge by drawing a bar of hardened steel swiftly along and across the square edge. A proprietary burnisher should be used for this, but you can improvise with the shaft of a screwdriver or any similar tool steel. The burr acts as the cutting edge and should be renewed whenever the scraper becomes difficult to work.

Concave, gooseneck and flat cabinet scrapers

# USING POWER SANDERS

Power sanders are most useful for the quick removal of waste stock before finishing by hand. A belt sander is worth considering if you have a lot of heavy-duty work, but does not produce an acceptable finish on its own. For general use, an orbital sander is by far the most versatile power tool to buy. When choosing a power sander, an important feature to look for is an efficient dust-collection facility. This not only reduces the amount of dust in the air, but also increases the working life of the machine and the sandpaper. Even with dust extraction, you should always use eye protection and a dust mask for your own health and safety.

## Belt sanders

A belt sander must be used with great care as the rotating belt removes large amounts of waste and you can easily create deep marks in the work, thus spoiling the piece. Keep the base moving constantly and always flat on the surface without forcing the machine. Its own weight will provide sufficient sanding pressure.

Use a belt sander to deal with uneven ridges in a laminated surface and for scouring off old paint finishes, but never use it for fine sanding and finishing work.

Always use the dust bag supplied with the belt sander, but preferably fit an adaptor to accept a dust extractor. You should empty the bag regularly to prevent the motor from overheating. Always wear a dust mask to prevent inhalation of dust particles, particularly if removing old paint, stains or varnish.

## Sanding belts

These sheets, like sandpaper, come in different grades, but the belts have a cloth backing for longer wear. They range from 40–60 grit (coarse grade) to 180 grit (extra fine). When fitting belts, look for the arrow printed inside, which indicates the direction of rotation.

1 Use the belt sander with a scouring action across the grain to level an uneven surface. The rotary action of the belt will tend to pull the work towards you, so clamp it firmly or use benchstops to prevent it from moving.

2 Using the same grade of belt, change direction to run the sander up and down the grain, removing the sanding marks running across the work. Change to a finer belt and repeat the process until the surface is flat.

## Multi-function sanders

Relatively new is a family of sanders with differently shaped base plates and attachments for sanding difficult profiles. They come with self-adhesive sanding pads, specially shaped to fit the triangular base. While very useful for cutting into corners and mouldings, they are not really suitable for heavy-duty work.

*Right and far right* The pads of these sanders fit easily into the corners of drawers and doors.

## Orbital sanders

As the name implies, an orbital sander moves the sanding pad in a circular motion for a much finer finish than a belt sander. It will still leave small circular marks on the work, however, which can only be removed by hand sanding with a sanding block. As the sandpaper collects more dust, the swirl marks tend to become more obvious, so change the paper regularly and use progressively finer grades, finishing up with 180 or 240 grit paper.

To prevent dust build-up, choose a model with a dust-collection bag that extracts dust from the surface of the wood through holes punched in the base as you work.

Orbital sanders are sold as half-sheet, third-sheet and quarter-sheet models. This allows you to cut a standard-sized sheet of sandpaper – 280 x 230mm (11 x 9in) – to fit the base without waste.

When buying sanding sheets, look for heavy-duty backing paper designed for use with power sanders. Aluminium oxide paper, sometimes called production paper, is by far the most durable and most efficient type.

1 Ready-sized sheets of sandpaper are available to fit each particular model, but they are more expensive. However, they do have the advantage of being pre-punched to allow dust extraction from the base. Some models are supplied with a small template for punching your own holes.

2 A small palm sander is ideal for the final finishing grades of paper. Work all over the surface with a series of overlapping circular motions, before finishing off with long strokes parallel to the grain.

3 The orbital sander in use is a much less ferocious cutter than a belt sander, and easier to control. The base plates are often made of foam rubber, which makes them gentle in use and more forgiving to the surface being worked on.

### Go with the grain

Always work "with the grain" when finishing wood – work along the wood fibres and in the direction in which they lie.

Study the edge of the timber (lumber) to obtain a clear picture before you begin. Sometimes the grain will change direction within the length of the same piece, so be prepared to change with it as you work.

On very coarse or uneven wood grain, there may be no easy solution – a block plane (right) set for a very fine cut can do the trick if used with a slicing action around difficult areas.

Alternatively, employ a cabinet scraper if you have one – it is well worth mastering the art of this simple tool.

✔ Work with the grain

✘ Not against the grain

Grain direction

# MAKING JOINTS

The basic techniques of woodworking are all that you need to begin to master the fine art of joinery. Patience, care and attention to detail provide the key to accurate joints; an understanding of how they work will allow you to choose the correct type for a given job. The techniques of joining wood have been developed over centuries, and there is satisfaction to be gained from employing these tried and tested methods. While it can be daunting to look at a long list of different joints with strange names, the following pages will demystify the whole subject. Ranging from the simplest of lap joints to more complex and decorative types, the joints shown cover most applications. As always, practice and good, sharp tools make perfect.

# Lap and Halving Joints

The simplest and most basic of joints is created where one piece of wood overlaps another. It is not the strongest method of joining two components, and may need reinforcing with extra fixings, but it is a straightforward technique. Where two pieces of the same thickness are to be connected, the strength of the joint can be greatly increased by forming a halving (half) joint.

## Corner lap joint

A typical use would be to form the corners of a drawer or simple box, where the shoulder of the joint adds strength and helps to keep the construction square.

*Right* The finished corner lap joint.

1 Mark out the thickness and depth of the lap with a scribing knife and gauge, then cut along the shoulder line with a tenon saw, keeping to the waste side of the line.

2 Clamp the piece firmly to the bench in a vice or use a G-clamp. Remove the waste wood with a series of small cuts, using a chisel and carpenter's mallet.

3 Pare down the wood to the scribed line with the chisel to complete the joint. Check the fit of the joint and make any fine adjustments. Pin and glue the joint together.

## Mitred halving joint

When glued and pinned from the underside, this more than doubles the strength of a simple mitred corner joint. Note that the end grain is revealed on one edge only.

*Above* The finished mitred halving joint.

1 Mark out a half lap and the depth of the join on the top half of the joint using a try square and pencil, then remove exactly half the thickness of wood. Pare down to the shoulder with a very sharp bevelled chisel.

2 Mark out the mitre on the top face of the lap and remove the waste with a tenon saw. Lay the finished piece over the lower section and use it as a guide for scribing the other half of the joint.

3 Cut along the shoulder line and remove waste wood by tapping gently with a chisel. Pare away the seat of the joint to make a snug fit. Glue the joint together.

## Cross-halved (half-lap) joint

This is the classic method of joining two intersecting pieces of equal thickness. Cut the shoulders accurately to form a very strong and square connection.

*Above* The completed cross-halved joint.

1 Mark the width of the bottom member on the underside of the top piece, then gauge the depth to half its thickness. Make a series of saw cuts across the waste area.

3 Pare down to the scribed lines using a bevel-edged chisel to ensure a flat and even seat for the joint. Hold the chisel blade perfectly horizontal and work toward the centre.

2 Remove the waste by chopping down sharply with a chisel to snap out small sections of waste at a time. This removes the risk of splitting the timber (lumber).

4 When the top half of the joint fits the bottom piece snugly, use it as a guide for scribing the exact width of the cut-out on the bottom half, then repeat steps 1–3.

## Lapped dovetail joint

An elegant means of creating a very strong joint that prevents one component from pulling away from another. It is useful for connecting rails and cross-members.

*Above* The finished lapped dovetail joint.

1 Cut the top half of the lap first, as for a straightforward lap joint. Use a bevel gauge to mark the dovetail on the top face.

3 Lay the finished dovetail over the lower piece to mark out the socket, and cut away the waste. Pare down to the scribed lines carefully with a shoulder plane to make a tight fit. Glue the joint together.

2 Clamp the work in a vice and cut down to the shoulders with a fine tenon saw. Remove the waste and pare down to the lines with a chisel.

# HOUSING AND BRIDLE JOINTS

**Another simple method of joining two pieces of wood where the end of one meets the side of the other is to cut a slot (housing) in the latter for the former. This provides positive location and strength.**

## Full housing joint

This is a simple means of joining two parts of a frame at right angles, for example where a cross-rail meets an upright. In this case, the full width of the rail is housed within the cut-out. You can also stop the housing short of the face side of the job.

*Above* The completed full housing joint.

1 The rail must be of a length that allows for the depth of the housing, and its end must be cut square. Use a vernier gauge to check the width of the rail accurately.

3 Use a sanding block, or an offcut (scrap) of wood wrapped with sandpaper (take care not to tear the paper), to trim the housing for a snug fit. Keep it absolutely flat to avoid rounding off the shoulders. You may have to plane the corresponding part of joint to make a good fit.

2 Use the other side of the vernier gauge to set the width of the housing. Scribe and cut the shoulders, then remove any waste to half the thickness of the rail.

## Bare-faced housing joint

When creating a housing joint in a corner, as for a door or window frame, leave an extra amount on the end of the cross-member for maximum strength. The bare-faced tenon on the upright is formed by removing waste from one side only.

1 Cut the shoulder for the tenon on the outer face. This puts the bare face on the inside of the joint to give a fixed internal measurement. Pare the tenon and shoulder to the scribed lines.

2 Set the two pins of a mortise gauge to match the width of the tenon you have made, then adjust the stock so that the housing groove will be positioned correctly.

## Bridle joint

A neat method of joining two components where they meet at a corner. This joint is versatile because it does not have to be a right angle and it is suitable for small sections. The tenon part of the joint is usually one-third of the thickness of the wood.

*Above* The completed corner bridle joint.

1 Use a mortise gauge to mark out the mortise, making it one-third of the thickness of the wood. Cut down to the required depth and chop out the waste with a chisel.

3 Clamp the tenon member firmly. Cut the shoulders of the joint with a tenon saw and remove the waste. Leave the tenon oversize at this stage for final fitting.

2 Without altering the mortise gauge setting, scribe the tenon to suit the mortise, making sure that you gauge from the face side of the wood. Shade the waste areas with a pencil.

4 Trial fit the joint by sliding both members together on a flat surface. This will indicate any high spots that need removing from the tenon for a flush fit.

3 Scribe the position of the housing with the mortise gauge, then mark the required depth for the tenon. Cut down to the lines with a tenon saw, and chisel out the waste.

*Above* The finished bare-faced housing joint.

# MORTISE AND TENON JOINTS

**These are some of the most useful joints you can master. They are the basis for most panelled doors, windows and joinery. The secret of success lies not so much in achieving a good fit for the tenon in the mortise, but rather in the accurate cutting of the shoulders of the tenon, which ensures a square and rigid construction when the joint is drawn up tight.**

### Basic mortise and tenon

The mortise and tenon joint has been adapted to meet a number of specific jointing needs, particularly to provide additional strength. The main types are shown here, and will prove useful as you develop your jointing skills.

Always cut the mortise first. Set the pins of a mortise gauge to suit a convenient size of chisel, about one-third the thickness of the wood.

1 Set the stock to centralize the mortise, and run the mortise gauge along the face side of the timber (lumber). Set the gauge aside without altering the setting of the pins – it will also be needed to mark out the thickness and the position of the tenon.

2 Drilling a row of holes between the gauged marks is a quick means of removing the majority of the waste. Use a spur-point drill bit (dowel drill bit) to ensure that the holes are kept in line. Make sure the holes are truly vertical – use a drill stand or pillar drill if possible.

3 Chop out most of the remaining waste from the mortise, then begin to pare down to the scribed lines with a broad chisel. Don't be hasty and try to remove too much at a time, otherwise you run the risk of splitting the wood along the grain.

4 Use a small chisel that matches the width of the mortise to chop out the ends. A firmer chisel can be used with a mallet to remove most of the waste. Finish off with a bevelled chisel, as shown, to get right into the corners for a perfectly square mortise.

5 Set out the tenon by marking the shoulder line with a carpenter's pencil on all sides. Use the mortise gauge to scribe the blade of the tenon, again working from the face side. Mark the waste to be removed with a saw and use a knife to scribe the cutting lines for the shoulders.

6 Cut across the grain at the shoulders with a fine-toothed tenon saw, keeping to the waste side of the scribed lines. Take care not to cut too deep, stopping just short of the scribed marks for the tenon blade. It is best to clamp the piece of work in a vice or with G-clamps for a positive hold.

7 Clamp the wood upright in a vice and remove the two outer sections, sometimes called tenon cheeks, again keeping to the waste side of the lines. Making sure that the wood is truly vertical will help you to produce straight cuts and taking time to cut accurately will save later adjustment.

8 Place the wood flat on the bench and pare down to the scribed marks. Use a paring chisel, pressing down on the blade with your forefinger to keep it absolutely horizontal. Try the tenon in the joint as you work, noting where it feels tight and paring gently until you achieve a perfect fit.

## Wedged-through tenon

By far the strongest form of mortise and tenon joint, in which the tenon passes right through the matching component and is locked in place with small wedges.

This method is often used for doors and windows where the frame has to endure a high degree of stress and movement. Gluing the wedges in place ensures that the joint will never come apart, even if the wood shrinks slightly as it dries.

1 A very slight angle for the wedge is all that's needed to lock the joint. Mark out the waste areas beyond the ends of the mortise, and start the cuts with the tip of a small dovetail saw.

2 Use a chisel to complete the bevels. Note how the angle has been marked on the outside of the rail to act as a visual guide. Use the same angle when cutting wedges from small offcuts (scraps) of wood.

3 Apply glue to the joint and fit the pieces together. Slowly tap the wedges into place, alternating from one to the other to draw the joint up square. Leave to set before trimming off the excess.

## Double tenon

Where you are joining a very wide component, such as the middle rail of a door, a continuous mortise would cause too much weakness in the receiving member. You can solve this problem by cutting two tenons side by side. The best door frames usually have mortise and tenon joints and they are frequently used in joinery and cabinet-making.

1 Form the double mortise in the usual way. If the tenons are 50mm (2in) wide, leave about the same distance between them. Pare the sides of each mortise.

2 It is more accurate to cut the tenon as a single piece, then remove the section in the middle. Pare down the shoulders. Clean up any waste with a chisel.

3 Fit the joint together. Both tenons should fit snugly into their mortises. Make sure there is a very small space for glue and then clamp when setting.

## Fox tenon

This variation is similar to the wedged tenon, but is used where the tenon is "blind" and does not pass completely through the receiving member.

It is an elegant and secret joint that will remain locked together. Great accuracy is required, though, because you only get one chance to assemble it. The size of the small "fox" wedges is critical.

1 Form a stopped mortise and tenon joint, then cut two slots about halfway down the length of the tenon. Note their positions – the idea is to force the edges of the tenon sufficiently outward to grip the inside of the mortise.

2 Cut two small wedges to such a size that, when the joint is assembled, the bottom of the mortise will drive them home and lock the joint. Set them in the slots, apply glue and fit the pieces together. Clamp them together while the glue dries and sets.

# DOVETAIL JOINTS

The dovetail joint is a fine example of the woodworker's art, combining a sound structural connection with a decorative appearance. You will come across many examples of furniture where dovetails have been used deliberately to display the cabinet-maker's pride in the work.

### Making a basic dowel joint

Accuracy and forethought are called for in setting out the joint correctly. The orientation of the dovetail determines how the components will be assembled.

1 Begin by setting out the "tails" of the joint from which the dovetail joint gets its name. The end of the tail member must be perfectly square, so be sure to use a shooting board and block plane to square up the end grain.

2 With hardwood, an angle of about 7 degrees (or pitch of 1:8) will ensure maximum strength from the joint without weakening the pins. Note how the waste at each end of the joint is roughly half the size of the gaps between the tails.

3 Always mark the waste areas between the tails as you work, because it's easy to become confused at this stage. Use a knife to scribe across the grain and mark the shoulder lines between the tails.

4 Clamp the work upright to make saw cuts for the tails, keeping to the waste side of the lines. Set the wood at an angle so that you hold the saw blade vertical for half the cuts, then reposition it to finish.

5 Use a coping saw to remove the waste from between the tails. Having the waste sections clearly marked out will prevent you from making any mistakes.

6 Turn the work horizontally to remove the last two portions of waste at the ends of the joint. Use a fine-toothed dovetail saw for this work.

7 Finally, use a bevelled chisel to pare down to the shoulder line and finish the tails. Work gradually towards the line, taking care to make the sides absolutely straight and square.

8 When marking out the pins, it helps to hold the work in a vice about 25mm (1in) proud. Highlight the end grain with a piece of chalk, especially on a dark hardwood such as the teak, used here.

9 Use the tails as a guide for marking out the positions of the pins. Place a block of scrap wood beneath the dovetail member so that it is square to and level with the pin member. Shade in the areas to be cut with a pencil.

10 Scribe the cut lines and shoulders for the pins with a knife, mark the waste sections, then remove them with a dovetail saw and chisel. Pare the pins to match the tails until the joint slides together smoothly.

## Varieties of dovetail joint

Over the years, cabinet-makers have developed many varieties of dovetail joint to suit different applications. After you have mastered the basic principle, try some of the other types. The lapped dovetail conceals the end grain of the tails, which are fitted into sockets in the pin member. You might find this in use on the front panel of a drawer. A mitred dovetail is even more challenging – both sections of end grain are concealed by mitred housings. Modern machine-made joints use more permanent adhesives than were available previously, so some of the more artful dovetails have fallen out of use. A comb joint is simple to machine, depending entirely on glue to form the bond, and it can look attractive.

*Above* The completed dovetail joint. The dovetails take their name from their fan shape and the pins form the top and the bottom of the joint and sit in between the tails. Sometimes the pins are smaller in width than the dovetails.

To ensure a good fit, the pins must be scribed accurately and directly off the corresponding part of the dovetail.

Lapped dovetail

Mitred dovetail

Comb joint

# ROUTERED JOINTS

A router is a powerful tool that comes into its own for making accurate joints, especially in large panels for carcass assembly. It is particularly useful for repetitive operations that demand a series of identical joints in several components. Accurate setting up and a methodical approach are essential for the best results. Always try out the router on a scrap of wood before starting on the work to ensure that the settings are correct.

### Housing joints

Routered housing joints are a simple means of locating shelves and dividers in a carcass. The housing is a groove that is precisely cut with a router to accept another piece of timber (lumber) at right angles to it. The strength of the joint depends on a tight and secure fit. The router will cut the shoulders and the base of the housing at the same time.

A stopped housing joint conceals the front edge of the joint from view.

1 Mark the end of the groove at the front edge. Work toward this end if possible, stopping the router cutter just short of the pencil line.

3 Cut out the rounded portion of waste at the end of the groove with a bevelled chisel.

4 Apply some glue to the bottom of the groove and slot the panel into position.

2 To prevent any breakout, use a knife to scribe the square end of the joint.

### Tongued-and-grooved housing

A router is useful for cutting continuous grooves accurately in long lengths of timber (lumber). This technique allows you to form the tongue to fit the groove exactly, whatever the thickness of timber.

1 Using the side fence of the router as a guide, rout a continuous groove in the first component.

2 Now form the tongue, gradually increasing the depth of cut until it is a perfect fit. Alternatively, you can purchase a matching cutter that forms the tongue in one pass of the router, but it is a lot more expensive and less versatile.

*Above* The finished tongued-and-grooved housing joint.

## Dovetailed housing

A dovetail profile cutter makes this self-locking joint easy to fabricate. There is no other practical way to form a long, dovetailed housing. To make a dovetail housing by hand would generally be too difficult and time-consuming.

The housing is of dovetail section. The corresponding part of the joint has a dovetail tongue. This type of joint has great structural strength. The dovetailer cannot be lowered into the work. The depth setting of the groove must be established before you begin working, and completed in one pass of the router.

1 Rout a square-section groove before using the dovetail cutter – this puts much less strain on the router and the cutter blades, as there is a lot of waste to remove.

2 Use a shoulder plane to trim the excess from the dovetail tongue to its finished size.

*Right* The finished dovetailed housing joint.

## Scribed joints

Profile cutters in matching pairs allow you to form perfectly fitted scribed joints for making panelled doors and mouldings.

1 When using scribing cutters, the depth setting is critical for a good match, so make sure you have a good supply of extra material of the same thickness to allow a few trial runs.

2 Machine the male portion of the moulding before forming the female half of the scribed joint. Work slowly and steadily to produce a smooth ripple-free finish.

3 The two profiles should match each other exactly. Slide them together on a flat surface to check for perfect alignment.

# Dowel Joints

Beech dowels offer a quick and simple means of strengthening corner joints and aligning two components to prevent them from twisting. Three common sizes are available: 6mm (¼in), 8mm (⁵⁄₁₆in) and 10mm (⅜in). Choose the diameter to suit the material – as a general rule, do not exceed half the thickness of the timber. There are several easy methods of locating them accurately.

### Centre-point method

Small brass or steel centre-points that match the dowel diameter come in dowelling kits that are available from hardware stores and also include a drill bit and dowels.

*Above* Dowels provide an invisible means of joining two sections of wood.

### Practical tip

The best dowels are slightly fluted to allow the glue to spread through the joint.

1 Use a dowel drill bit, also called a spur-point bit, to centre each hole accurately. A strip of tape wrapped around the bit makes a simple depth gauge. Hold the drill truly vertical – use a drill stand or pillar drill if you have a lot of holes to drill.

2 Insert the centre-points in the holes and simply push the adjacent component toward them, making sure that it is in its correct position. Use a square to check that the edges are flush.

3 Clamp the second piece in a vice and drill to the correct depth for the dowel.

4 Apply glue to the dowels, insert in the holes and tap the joint together.

### Dowel drilling jig

Slightly more expensive than a centre-point kit, but well worth the investment if you are making a lot of joints, the dowel drilling jig comes in several forms. The type illustrated offers a choice of bushes to take three sizes of dowel drill.

1 Mark the components carefully to ensure the correct orientation in the drilling jig. Clamp the two components together with the jig, making sure that the outer faces are touching.

2 Tape the bit to allow for the depth of the drilling bush. Drill the end grain of the first part. Without altering the position of the jig, drill the matching hole(s) in the second part.

3 Apply glue to the dowel and the face of the joint, and simply push together.

# BISCUIT JOINTS

**"Biscuit" is the term for a flat wafer of compressed hardwood, usually beech, that acts in the same way as a dowel. However, it must be fitted into a slot cut with a biscuit jointer. Again, they are available in three common sizes: size 0 (16mm/⅝in), size 10 (20mm/¾in) and size 20 (25mm/1in). The biscuits are baked to a low moisture content so that when water-based glue is applied, they swell and make a tight joint – store them in a sealed container to keep them dry.**

### Edge joints

The beauty of biscuit jointing is that marking out is easy – simply place the two components together in their intended positions and make a series of pencil marks at suitable intervals.

1 To make a simple plinth, cut the components to size and align them for marking out, ensuring that all the edges are flush.

2 Clamp each side upright in a vice to cut the slot. The reference mark on the jointer automatically centres it on the pencil mark.

3 Cut a slot for the other half of the joint by clamping the piece to the bench. It must be held firmly as you plunge the cutting blade into the wood.

4 To cut slots for biscuits in a mitred corner joint, simply adjust the jointer's scale to 45 degrees and proceed as before. A spacing block is sometimes needed to position the carriage at the correct height.

5 Clear any sawdust from the slots before inserting the biscuits. Coat each with a small amount of glue and tap into place.

6 Apply glue to the faces of the joints and fit the parts together. Apply clamping pressure to pull everything tight – an easy, fast and accurate system.

### Mitred joints

A simple frame with mitred corners can be reinforced with biscuits if the components are thick enough to accommodate them. The versatile jointing machine can save time and improve accuracy in a multitude of applications.

1 A mitre saw will cut the timber (lumber) easily and accurately.

2 Use a try square to align the corners accurately when marking.

3 The oval shape of the biscuit automatically centres the mitred joint as it fits together.

# JOINING BOARDS AND KNOCK-DOWN FITTINGS

**Manufactured sheet materials are available in large sizes, but occasionally it is necessary to join them together neatly. Because they lend themselves to machine-made joints, there are several options to choose from. Knock-down (K-D) fittings are used extensively in the furniture industry for manufacturing self-assembly units. They are useful for furniture that needs to be reassembled.**

## Lap joint

A lap joint is easily made with a router and is useful when matching veneered boards to make decorative panels.

1 Use a router fitted with a fence to form the lap, cutting it to exactly half the thickness of the material.

2 Apply glue and clamp the boards together. When the veneers are well matched, the seam will be almost invisible to the eye.

## Loose-tongue joint

An even stronger bond can be achieved by using a "loose tongue", which acts as a key for the adhesive. This type of joint takes little time to fabricate.

1 Use 6mm (¼in) plywood for a loose tongue. The cross-ply structure is stronger in bending than a long-grained section of hardwood. Apply glue and insert into a routed groove.

2 Firmly clamp the two panels flat to the bench before applying longitudinal pressure to the joint. This will keep it perfectly flat and produce a strong bond.

## Scarf joint

Two plywood panels can be joined with a feather-edged scarf joint, which will provide a large surface area for the glue. When made correctly, this type of joint will allow the completed panel to be formed into a curve without the joint separating or kinking.

1 This joint can be made easily with hand tools. Make up a simple jig on the workbench to control the angle of the plane.

2 Before clamping the joint together, drive in a few panel pins (brads) to prevent the boards from sliding around. Remove them when the glue has dried.

## Cam fittings

A cam fitting forms a solid connection by a single turn of a screwdriver, which locks a lever arm into place on the mating part of the joint. Such joints allow you to prefabricate a set of components and insert the fittings in the knowledge that they will automatically line up when assembled.

1 Drill a hole in each component for the two halves of the fitting. The exact dimensions for their size and location will be supplied with the fittings. Insert them in the holes.

2 Simply locate the peg of one half of the fitting in the matching hole of the other and turn the cam to lock the joint together.

## Construction screws

These special screws have an extremely coarse thread that is designed to grip the fibres in chipboard panels without splitting them – a common problem when using ordinary wood screws.

### Jointing blocks

This is a modern substitute for the traditional glued wooden block, allowing panels to be dismantled easily. Simply screw the block to each panel.

1 A drilling jig will be supplied with the screws. Drill a clearance hole in the outer panel to suit the shank size of the screw.

2 Using the same jig, drill a pilot hole of smaller diameter into the end of the second panel. A depth stop on the drill bit will allow the depth of the hole to be controlled. Note how the jig locates the hole automatically. Assemble the panels by driving in the screws.

## Panel connectors

When joining large sections of worktop, for example, a positive mechanical connection will hold them tightly together, but still allow the two parts to be dismantled if necessary.

1 Drill a hole in each panel for the connector boss, using a hinge boring bit. Mark out a slot for the bolt, as shown, and cut down with a tenon saw. Remove any waste with a chisel.

2 Align the panels, using dowels or biscuits if desired, and tighten the connecting bolt until the joint is rigid. to the required depth.

# SCRIBING JOINTS

**"Scribing" can be a confusing term. It is often used to describe the marking out of a piece of wood with a sharp knife, but it also specifically refers to the method of transferring the shape of one piece of wood on to another. The latter is a particularly useful technique when working with mouldings of complex profile.**

## Using a profile gauge

A profile gauge incorporates a large number of plastic "fingers" that are free to move independently in the body of the gauge. When pressed against a moulded surface, they duplicate its profile, allowing this to be transferred to another component.

1 Place the moulding on a flat surface, hold the gauge level and press down slowly to achieve an accurate profile.

2 Square across the back of the second piece of moulding to provide a base line, then position the gauge and transfer the contours of the moulding with a pencil.

3 Mitre the end of the moulding back to the base line, which gives you a pattern to follow over the moulded surface. Follow this pattern with a coping saw, using the outline on the reverse side to keep the saw straight.

4 Clean up the cut with a gouge until the moulding is a perfect fit. Pare away small shavings at a time to prevent the end grain breaking away.

## Scribing by hand

On less complex shapes, a simple method is to use a scribing block. Any suitable scrap of wood can be used as a spacer to follow the shape.

1 Grip a pencil against the scribing block and run it down the surface to transfer the outline on to the adjoining piece.

*Left* The finished scribing joint.

2 Cut down the line with a coping saw. The result is a neat fit between the two pieces.

# Using Mouldings and Trims

Small sections of decorative moulding can be used to form joints and to add solid wooden edges to manufactured boards and panels. Ready-made mouldings, in a number of different shapes and sizes, are commonly available, and you can usually match solid hardwood trim to the veneered boards used for shelves and carcass work.

## Adding and gluing mouldings

1 Use a length of triangular moulding, sometimes called arris rail, to make a neat connection at an internal corner. This is more discreet than a square section of batten. Match the trim to the material you are working with.

2 Here, the arris moulding has been used to form the corner, leaving both edges of the panels exposed. Complete the joint with a section of scotia glued and pinned into the external corner.

3 If the moulding is thick enough, you can use biscuits to strengthen the joint and hold the moulding flush to one edge. This will provide extra stiffness to a shelf as well as concealing the exposed edge.

4 Finish off with small panel pins (brads), concealing their heads in the moulding detail. Set them in with a nail punch.

## Adding pre-glued veneers

1 Pre-glued edging strip can be obtained in a variety of types to suit veneered boards. It is simply applied by pressing into position with a hot iron. Keep the iron moving to avoid local discolouration.

2 Leave the glue to harden (no more than half an hour is needed), then remove the excess veneer. Wrap some fairly coarse sandpaper around a block of wood and use it with a slow knifing action to cut away the veneer.

# WOOD FINISHING

**A**pplying a perfect finish to your work may seem to be the last stage in the construction process, but the secret of success is to consider it from the very beginning. From the moment you conceive an idea and determine its design, the finish will influence all your subsequent decisions. Some species of wood are better suited to certain types of finishing materials; conditions of use will dictate the degree of durability and water resistance required.

The orientation of each component and its grain pattern, the types of joint and glue, the tools and techniques used, even the order of work and assembly, will be affected by the demands of the finishing process. Keeping this in mind will help to focus your work, and will require great discipline and forethought. The visual appeal of the material is one of the attractions of woodworking, and the art of finishing is to display that to the best advantage.

# FINISHING EQUIPMENT

There is a wide choice of finishes for your work, from materials that have been tried and tested over hundreds of years to modern products formulated to meet the demands of the furniture industry. Compared to the cost of timber, finishing materials are not that expensive, which allows you to experiment with every project to perfect your techniques and discover the features of each method. For a small outlay, you can assemble the basic equipment to get started, then add to this as you progress.

## Preparation

The key to a good result, as always, lies in careful preparation. When a glossy finish is applied to a surface, small scratches or blemishes will be revealed that previously were barely visible to the naked eye. There is no substitute for a methodical approach, working through progressively finer grades of abrasive paper until you cannot feel any improvement.

A word of warning, though – your fingers can transmit greasy deposits and damp patches to the surface, so keep your hands clean and handle

fine items with great care. Pick them up by the edges, or wear disposable gloves. Stack the finished components on clean softwood battens (cleats).

Carry out preparation work well away from the finishing area, and be prepared to move the work back and forth several times as you apply and rub down successive coats. Assemble a good supply of clean rags, wire (steel) wool, abrasive paper and scraping tools. Even used sheets of abrasive paper come in useful, as they lose some of their cutting ability and produce a progressively finer finish.

### Workshop conditions

A suitable area in which to work is a priority. Sanding activities create dusty conditions, and dust is the enemy of a fine finish. It is best to work in a separate room, well away from the woodworking area. If you do not have this luxury, seal off an area of the main workshop with plastic sheeting or a partition. Organize your work so that you carry out finishing on a separate day, and keep away while each coat is drying.

Most finishing materials depend on the evaporation of solvents as they cure, so the area should be well ventilated, but you should prevent draughts and maintain a controlled temperature to ensure ideal drying conditions. Install good lighting, and position the finishing bench in the centre of the room so that you can move around your work without moving it. Drying racks fixed to the wall will be good for stacking small components.

### Dealing with blemishes

If you find a small blemish in your work at a late stage, all is not lost. There are various filling and stopping compounds, some of which are better than others. Soft interior stopping is fine for tiny cracks, and comes in a range of pre-mixed colours to suit different wood species. You can blend these together or add a drop of wood stain to match the wood's colour and tone, but check first that the stain you

*Above, clockwise from top left* Wire (steel) wool, filler, spatula, soft cloth, sanding block, abrasive papers and cabinet scrapers.

use is compatible with the final finish. Larger holes may need filling with a hard-setting exterior-grade filler. Leave this just proud of the surface, as it tends to shrink as it cures, then sand it flush. Shrinkage is a disadvantage of many fillers, which can shrink further and even fall out of the wood.

### Health and safety

Many substances that are used for finishing are flammable or contain ingredients that are hazardous. Keep them in a lockable area, out of the reach of children and preferably out of doors. Always keep containers sealed, and observe the manufacturers' instructions for the safe use of the materials. Do not pour used solvents or thinners into a domestic drainage system – take them to a safe disposal site at your local recycling centre. Old paintbrushes, rags and polishing cloths can also be hazardous – do not leave them lying around or mix them with other waste.

## Brushes

You get what you pay for when buying brushes. Keep a stock of cheap disposable brushes for building up coats of primer and sealer – sometimes the price of thinners for cleaning a brush outweighs the cost of a new one. However, for finish coats, invest in good-quality brushes and keep them separate for different applications to avoid contamination. Clean them every time you use them, wash out in warm soapy water, and store them dry and in a dust-free container. A quality brush improves with age as the bristles become "worked in".

*Right (Top row)* 75mm (3in) disposable brush; 100mm (4in) lacquering brush; 50mm (2in), 38mm (1½in) and 12mm (½in) full-bodied paintbrushes. *(Bottom row)* Polishing mops and a variety of artist's brushes.

## Shellac stopping

More traditional forms of filler, ideal for restoration work, can be obtained from specialist suppliers. Shellac stopping comes in stick form and a useful colour range. It sets quite hard and bonds well to the wood with minimal shrinkage.

1 During restoration of this table top, the removal of an old coat of varnish revealed a large knot. This was not unattractive, but needed to be treated and sealed before the application of a new finish. A cabinet scraper was used first to cut back the fibrous material around the knot.

2 The very centre of the knot had dried out and formed a small hole. The tip of the shellac stick was melted with an old soldering iron, and the small drops were allowed to fill the hole and soak into the wood surrounding the knot.

3 When the filler had hardened, the excess was scraped away with a sharp chisel until it was flush with the surface. More stopping was applied as necessary; several layers would be required for a deep blemish.

4 Wax filler was then rubbed over the areas of rough grain surrounding the knot. This sealed the entire surface and it should prevent further shrinkage of the wood.

5 The table top was smoothed with extra-fine sandpaper (320 grit) on a cork sanding block, using small circular motions at first, followed by working along the grain direction.

6 The entire surface was wiped down with a soft damp cloth, using long strokes parallel to the grain. This removed all final traces of dust and served to raise the grain slightly by adding moisture. When dry, it was rubbed down again with 400 grit paper before finishing.

# STAINING

Stained and polished wood will be familiar to anyone who has seen antique furniture, such as "Jacobean" oak or mahogany from the 19th century. The use of wood stain is less fashionable today, the accent being on letting the natural colour of the material speak for itself. However, the purpose of staining is not always to make the wood appear darker. Creative use of a wood stain can enhance a grain pattern that otherwise would appear bland. With care, you can use very dilute stains to match different components in a construction, or to achieve attractive contrasts of tone. Even quite strong colours can be used to striking effect for a contemporary look on wooden toys and furniture.

## Types of stain

Ready-mixed wood stains are readily available from all good hardware stores and paint suppliers, but care is necessary to ensure that the type of stain is compatible with the finish. All three common types have their advantages and disadvantages.

The colour of wood stain is often labelled according to wood species: pine, mahogany or oak, for example. This can be very misleading, as the result depends on the base colour of the wood to which it is applied. Always test the stain you want to use on an offcut (scrap) of the same piece of wood first and let it dry thoroughly. Apply a coat of the chosen finish over the stain to make sure that there is no reaction between solvents.

## Bleaching

Bleaching is a technique that can be used to revive an old piece of wood or correct a patchy appearance. It can even out defects in the wood's appearance before more stain is applied. Always be careful when handling chemicals – wear heavy-duty rubber gloves, overalls and eye protection. Most wood bleach is applied as a two-part treatment. The base coat is washed into the grain, then the activator is added to set up the chemical reaction. Small bubbles appear on the surface and a noticeable colour change should be visible after 15–20 minutes. Rinse with plenty of water, or the required neutralizer, then sand down when dry. Some species of

wood, particularly oily varieties such as teak and rosewood, are not easy to bleach; mahogany, beech and light oak produce better results. Always test bleach on an offcut or concealed area of the workpiece before committing yourself.

## Fuming

Fuming is another application of chemistry to the art of finishing. Wood with a high acid content, oak in particular, will react with ammonia gas and turn a deep rich brown. Not being a surface stain, the colour is fixed in the material. The process is particularly useful for treating an entire piece of furniture that has many detailed parts, which would make applying stain difficult. Ordinary household bleach contains ammonia, although more consistent results can

*Above* Different types and colours of stain, here being tested on strips of pine.

be obtained from a stronger solution. You can build a simple fuming chamber by constructing a light framework that is large enough to contain the object, then covering it with thin plywood or hardboard. Seal all the joints with plastic tape, then place the item inside with a wide, shallow container of ammonia solution. Handle the container with great care, making sure you do not splash the liquid on to any exposed skin. Wear gloves, goggles and protective clothing, and work in a well-ventilated area, preferably outdoors in a sheltered spot. Seal the chamber and leave for at least 24 hours. The amount of darkening depends on the exposure time allowed.

### Applying wood stain

Wear a pair of disposable latex gloves to protect your hands, particularly when working with a solvent-based stain. This also prevents the workpiece from being marked by the oils in your hands when you move it. Shake the container well, and if you have mixed up your own blend, make sure that you have prepared enough to complete the job.

1 Use a small brush to test the colour or to apply small patches of stain to even out any pale areas of the wood. Dilute the stain when treating the end grain of timber, which is more absorbent and will take too much stain, leading to a darker finish.

2 With a soft cloth or ready-made staining pad, apply the stain with quick circular motions, keeping the pad fully charged. For an even coat, the wood should absorb as much stain as possible while it is still wet.

3 Before the stain has completely dried, rub the pad along the surface with long strokes up and down the grain to remove any excess colour.

### Touching up

You can use a small watercolour brush to match the grain pattern of highly figured wood. Here, a small piece of veneer has lifted after the staining process.

1 Add a drop of stain to a small amount of stopping that matches the lighter background. Apply this to the damaged area with a spatula or modelling knife.

2 Rub down the repair very gently and dab with a light stain to blend it in. When dry, mix up a darker stain and copy the grain pattern with a fine-tipped brush.

3 The completed repair becomes almost undetectable when the finish coat is applied.

## Wood stains

### Water-based stains

**Pros:** Low in cost, safe to use and contain no harmful solvents. They are non-toxic and taint-free, and suitable for wooden toys, food utensils, storage units or items where safety is paramount.

**Cons:** These can produce uneven or patchy results, are slow drying and have poor penetration on oily and resinous woods. Not always colour-fast and can fade in strong sunlight. They will raise the grain of some woods, especially softwoods.

### Solvent-based stains

**Pros:** These are quick drying; they use methylated spirit as a solvent. They will not raise the grain and can be inter-mixed successfully, or mixed with shellac sealer or polish to add body to further coats. Light-fast stains have a long life.

**Cons:** These require fast work to prevent blotchy results and variations in finish due to overlapping. They are not compatible with cellulose lacquers.

### Oil-based stains

**Pros:** These come in a range of pre-mixed strong colours and are easy to apply evenly. Only one coat is required: further applications of stain tend to lift the first coat.

**Cons:** These are difficult to dilute or mix to create your own colours. They are not compatible with white spirit-based finish coats or wax polish. They give mixed results on close-grained wood.

# VARNISH, PAINT AND LACQUER

For a hard wearing and waterproof finish, a coat of clear varnish takes some beating. Traditional, oil-based varnish is not ideal for finishing wood, as the resins in the varnish give an orange cast to the film and can obscure the natural colours of the wood.

Of the more modern varnishes, polyurethane is easier to apply and produces a clearer result. It requires white spirit (turpentine) as a solvent and is safe to use with the normal precautions. Acrylic varnish is water-based, less toxic and quick drying, but it is less hard wearing in the long run.

Lacquers tend to be much thinner and require a build-up of several coats to be effective. The best results are obtained by spray application, which is not always a practical proposition for the home woodworker. Cellulose solvents for lacquer are quite unpleasant and flammable at lower temperatures.

### Preparation

Varnish needs a good key to the wood surface to prevent blistering and peeling. On oily wood, apply a coat of shellac sanding sealer beforehand, as this will improve adhesion. Alternatively, apply a priming coat of varnish diluted with 50 per cent white spirit (turpentine), allowing it to soak well into the grain of the wood. Leave to dry for 24 hours before rubbing down lightly with fine sandpaper.

### Paint

While the benefits of a natural wood finish are undeniable, good paintwork also has its place. The brushing technique is much the same as for clear varnish and demands the same care in preparation. On very resinous and coarse-grained wood, apply a priming coat of shellac sanding sealer before painting to prevent patchy drying and cracking of the paint film. Continue with primer and several undercoats until the surface is smooth before applying the topcoat. Although paint is opaque, it will not necessarily mask unsightly blemishes.

Painted furniture and other woodwork is a subject in its own right, offering a wide choice of paint effects to explore. You can experiment with acrylic paints and glazes, which bond well to wood and can be used to good effect as tinted backgrounds with all manner of decorative touches.

Always seal the wood with a topcoat of clear lacquer to protect the finished paintwork.

### Common finishing faults and their causes

#### Patchy areas in the finish coat
Uneven sanding of the surface during preparation
Oil or grease contamination

#### Ridges or ripples
Varnish drying too quickly as you join up the brush strokes – work on a smaller area at a time; check that the room temperature is not too high

#### "Orange peel" effect – small pinholes in a rough surface
Varnish applied too thickly in each coat
Uneven drying

#### "Bloom" – milky-white colour in the film
Presence of moisture on the surface or in the brush
Damp atmosphere or cold draughts

#### Crazing – small surface cracks developing in the glaze
Applying coats too rapidly without leaving time to dry
Using incorrect solvents that react with a stain or sealing coat

*Top right* The carcass of this display case was made from medium-density fibreboard, which was painted after assembly.
*Left* This table was finished with several coats of clear lacquer, rubbing down carefully between each coat for a mirror finish.

## Varnishing technique

Use a good-quality brush with a full head of bristles, making sure that it is clean. Small flecks of dust or dried varnish in the brush will tend to loosen as you work and ruin the job. Pour a quantity of varnish, sufficient for one coat, into a small container and reseal the tin at once to prevent a skin from forming. Dip the brush no more than halfway into the varnish and avoid overloading it. Drips and runs are the most common causes of a poor finish.

1 If treating a complex piece of work, such as this panelled door, always begin with the fine detail. Use a small brush to work along the edges of mouldings and panelling, brushing out any build-up in the corners.

2 Change to a larger brush for the wider areas of panelling, using long strokes. Hold the brush at an angle to the surface and work quickly, but carefully. Pay attention to the V-grooves, which can trap small runs of varnish.

3 Support the work on small clean battens (cleats) to lift it clear of the finishing table. This allows treatment of the outer edges. Try not to overload the brush here – too much varnish will creep down and collect on the underside.

4 Move to the main members of the panel, treating the cross-rails first. Brush along the grain.

5 Finish off by brushing up and down the vertical stiles of the door, picking up the brush strokes at the ends of the rails and brushing out well along the grain. When dry, turn the door over and coat the other side in the same way before rubbing down.

6 Use 000 grade fine wire (steel) wool to remove any nibs of varnish on mouldings and edges. Brush the debris well clear to remove small fragments of wire wool, which easily become trapped in the corners.

7 Rub down all the flat surfaces with 320 grit silicon carbide paper until the first coat of varnish is silky smooth. For a quality finish, repeat the entire operation four or five times, building up a really flat and well-keyed surface.

8 Apply the final coat with a fine-haired polishing mop. If the surface is really smooth, this requires no effort and can be carried out very quickly, avoiding any streaks and ridges, for a mirror finish.

# FINISHING WITH WAX AND OIL

Wax has been used as a treatment for finishing wood for centuries, and it is still very much in favour. Whereas a coat of varnish has to bond to the wood and provide a separate protective layer, wax sinks into the surface and produces a deep, lustrous finish that improves with age. Less skill is required for its application, and it is easy to refresh and renew. Oil is even more straightforward to use, and some modern formulations have the advantage of being slightly more durable and heat-resistant. No special equipment is needed to apply wax or oil, other than a soft cloth and fine wire (steel) wool.

### Types of wax

Pure beeswax is a natural product that provides a wonderful finish for fine furniture. However, it is less durable than other types and can soften in warm temperatures.

The most common wax for wood is carnauba wax. It is much harder than pure beeswax – a mixture of the two can be successful. It is more resistant to wear, but more difficult to apply.

Beware of using silicone-based "wax polish" as a natural wood treatment. It is quick to apply and produces a glossy finish, but when this wears off, the result is patchy and dull. It attracts a build-up of dust and dirt, and is difficult to refresh. Silicone is not compatible with any other type of finish and is impossible to remove.

Furniture wax can be obtained ready coloured to suit different wood types. It will not act as a stain on its own, but over time will build up a deep lustrous colour within the wood surface. It can be applied safely over a spirit wood stain, but can cause problems with oil-based stain. On soft wood with open grain, it helps to seal the wood beforehand. When you are working on very dense, close-grained wood, warm the wax beforehand over a low heat, such as above a radiator. Finish off by rubbing along the grain and leave it for an hour or two to settle.

*Left, clockwise from top left* There are many different types and colours of wax for polishing woodwork and furniture: liming wax, carnauba wax, teak oil, soft cloth, wax filler sticks, beeswax, solid beeswax.

1 Apply a thin coat of sanding sealer or clear shellac. This provides a stable base for the wax, but does not prevent it from sinking deep into the grain. When dry, rub down very lightly with worn pieces of fine sandpaper and brush off.

2 Apply the wax with a ball of fine wire (steel) wool. The wax lubricates the cutting action and prevents too much abrasion, while being forced deep into the wood fibres. Use a strong circular motion to work the wax well in. The harder you work, the more friction is created, which softens the wax further.

3 Form a polishing pad from a soft duster and buff the wax vigorously. Add two or three more thin coats as the wax settles, then continue to build up the finish. To refresh a polished wax finish, first wash with warm soapy water to remove any debris. If the finish is really soiled, clean it with fine wire wool moistened with white spirit (turpentine). Add another coat of wax.

## Liming wax

A limed finish can be very attractive, particularly on oak and other wood with a strong grain figure. The white liming paste penetrates the grain and provides pleasing highlights. Over time, the lime continues to react with the acid content of the wood to produce a deep lustre.

*Above* A coat of liming wax accentuates the grain of the wood beautifully.

1 Apply a coat of sanding sealer. When it is dry, work the liming wax into the grain with fine wire (steel) wool. Use a circular motion, as you would for normal wax, but do not finish off along the grain. This would tend to lift the wax from the grain.

2 Wipe the excess wax away with firm strokes directly across the grain. Use a soft mutton cloth with a coarse weave for the best result. Leave to dry for about four hours, then buff with a soft cloth. Seal with clear lacquer, or add more clear wax for a silky finish.

## Oil treatment

Oil is a natural waterproofer and, as such, is the perfect finish for outdoor furniture, especially on oily woods such as teak. It will outlast any varnish treatment, without the risk of water penetrating the film and causing it to lift, which is a common problem with exterior varnish. The correct oil will dry to form a protective film, but can be cut back and enriched by adding another coat at any time.

Linseed oil is not an ideal choice, as it remains soft and attracts the build-up of dust. Boiled linseed oil will form a protective crust, but is not heat-resistant and can become tacky in warm weather. Teak oil and Danish oil contain mineral extracts that help to preserve wood. They are more durable and are the best choice. One word of caution: oil is sometimes used to finish wooden culinary utensils and salad bowls. Clearly, metallic-based oils are not suitable for such items, so use thin vegetable oil instead.

1 Application of an oil finish could not be easier. Remove all traces of dust from the surface and work in the oil with fine wire (steel) wool. Allow it to soak in and, if uneven patches are visible, keep applying more until the wood achieves a uniform colour.

2 Finish off with long strokes up and down the grain, using a very soft cloth to work in the oil well. Leave it to dry overnight.

# INDEX

**Picture credits**
DIY Photo Library p28br; p29br. Forest Life Picture Library pp6tr, bl; 10tr, 11tl, b; 21cl. Imagebank p14b. Liz and John Boddy p14tr; 15tr, br; 18c.

The publisher would like to thank FSC for allowing the reproduction of their logo on page 20, and Graham Bruford at Forests Forever for permission to reproduce text on page 21.

# NOTES

# Notes